RON SCHARA'S

MINNESOTA BOUND

With "Raven" Star of "Minnesota Bound"

TRISTAN OUTDOORS

Minneapolis

TRISTAN OUTDOORS is an Imprint of TRISTAN Publishing, Inc.

TRISTAN OUTDOORS
2355 Louisiana Avenue North
Golden Valley, Minnesota 55427
www.tristanoutdoors.com

TRISTAN Publishing, Inc. believes that the following information is accurate; however, we cannot guarantee or accept liability for the accuracy. The information within this book has been provided by Ron Schara Enterprises.

Cover Photographs by Lee Thomas Kjos

To my late Grandpa Clate Dickens, who loved telling stories as much as I loved to hear them. As they say, what you live with, you learn.

To my wife, Denise and daughters, Simone and Laura, for years of listening patiently to my tales. And to grandson Jake who has yet to hear all of them.

To my assistant, Kelly McDonnell, who has guided me and this book project in both rough and calm waters.

And, lastly, to my colleagues at Minnesota Bound who aimed the cameras, who recorded the scripts and who, through the editing process, brought each story to life for the viewers of Minnesota Bound.

TABLE OF CONTENTS

■ INTRODUCTION

■ MAGICAL PLACES

■ SAVING THE LAND

MEET MOTHER NATURE

UNFORGETTABLE FOLKS

■ WHERE THE FISH ARE

HUNTING TALES

MY PASSION: WILD TURKEYS

MEMORABLE MOMENTS

For more than a decade, thousands of Minnesotans have tuned in their television sets to watch a show known as **Minnesota Bound**. A black lab with a red bandana is the star. Her name is **Raven**. I'm the guy on the other end of the leash.

I'm also lucky. A long time ago I tried to produce a television show about the great outdoors. The only thing great was the amount of money I lost. My wife, Denise, said I was done with that dream.

A few years later, the news director at KARE-11 television called and asked if I would be willing to do a few outdoor stories for them. I said I would. The stories were called Minnesota Bound.

Somebody suggested that, instead of a two minute feature, Minnesota Bound should be a regular half hour show. I thought it was a great idea. The station manager was cautious. He offered me a 13 week contract. No more. Can you produce the show, he asked? Yes, I lied. I didn't even know how to find the on switch on a video camera and I wasn't sure what beta tape was.

On a February Sunday, Minnesota Bound made its debut, under the guidance of senior producer, Joe Harewicz.

If there's such a thing as an instant hit, Minnesota Bound was it. And it still is.

I'm often asked to explain the success of Minnesota Bound. Frankly, I'm not sure. Most television shows, including the really good ones, seldom last but a few years. It's the nature of the television entertainment business.

So, why has Minnesota Bound stayed on KARE-11, the NBC affiliate, for so many seasons, airing twice a week, and attracting tens of thousands of viewers on a weekly basis?

One reason is John Remes, the station manager at KARE, who was committed to local programming. In the days when we needed production assistance, John made available technical assistance from the station's staff and allowed us to purchase beta tapes at a discount.

A second reason is I had graduated from the TV school of hard knocks and was ready to try again. You'll recall my lost shirt the first time I tried to be a television producer. Despite the setbacks, I was convinced that the field of outdoor television programming was a huge opportunity.

Most fishing or hunting shows are often versions of home movies where the host simply demonstrates what a wonderful angler he is, catch after catch, until yet another fish on the line becomes video boredom. A half-hour show with nothing on the screen but catching fish or shooting birds is an insult to the wonderful world of hunting and fishing.

State of Minnesota Proclamation
Ron Schara, Raven, & Minnesota Bound Day,
Thursday, May 13th 2004

What was missing, in my opinion, was a journalistic treatment to outdoor programming by including the who, what, where, when, in addition to the how.

Today, Minnesota Bound and other television shows are produced by Ron Schara Enterprises, including some of the most talented TV folks in the Twin Cities. They are: Miss Kelly, my right arm; Steve Plummer, Mike Cashman, Aaron Achtenberg, Nick Clausen, Bill Sherck, Jared Christie, Brian Maginnis and Don Stremski. And, yes, Joe Harewicz, who produced the first Minnesota Bound is still pumping them out, too.

My two daughters, Simone and Laura, and lovely wife, Denise, also have worked on productions. Simone does the bookkeeping. Laura hosts a wild in the city segment. Denise... well, she's everybody's mother hen.

Along with Raven, we also were smart enough to feature Belinda Jensen, everybody's girl next door and a talented one.

As for me, well, I still pinch myself. Minnesota Bound's incredible run shows no end in sight.

The Family: Ron, Denise, Laura and Simone Schara

Today if you ask me why, I have an answer. Our viewers told us over the years what they like.

My answer is this: we are storytellers. And from the days of cavemen, people have enjoyed stories. We also have met some of the most interesting folks in the outdoors. Each story is the actual script from the show along with still photos captured from the Minnesota Bound video.

Thanks for watching. And reading.

Did Somebody Mention Bloopers?

Well, yes, we've had a few. When you work with a dog, you get bloopers.

When you hang around rivers and mountains and wild turkeys and, well, the great outdoors, you end up with bloopers on video tape.

We've shared some bloopers over the years. The one and only time I've operated one of our video cameras was to record the firing of an elephant gun. My senior producer, Joe Harewicz, and I were roaming the wilds of South Africa and Zimbabwe, when our PH (that's African lingo for Professional Hunter/Guide) showed us his elephant gun. I can't recall the caliber or model but the rifle was heavy in the barrel and the bullet was thicker than a farmer's finger. We were marveling at the size of such a weapon when Joe said he'd like to take a shot so he could say he'd fired an elephant gun.

I kindly offered to record the moment.

On the count of three, Joe pulled the trigger. A former linebacker for Michigan State University, my senior producer is no wimp. Yet, when the elephant gun fired, the next thing I saw was Joe flying backwards as if he'd been hit by, well, a charging elephant. Sadly, the camera operator failed to record the entire episode (Joe's face covered with fear) so I decided to retire as a videographer.

One of Raven's biggest bloopers happened in a big place, the Mall of America. No camera was present. And that was a good thing. Early in our television career, Raven and I were headed for an appearance at the Mall of America. Frankly, I never considered the idea that Raven may have needed a potty break before entering the giant mall. Well, to make an embarrassing story short, I suddenly noticed a tug on Raven's leash and quickly realized Raven was not walking but squatting.

There we were: a huge mess on the floor with no means to clean it up.

At that moment in our desperation, from around a corner walks a Mall Security Officer with a shiny badge on his chest and a scowl on his face. He looked at Raven (no dogs are allowed in the Mall, normally) and then looked at me. I smiled. He didn't. He asked, "What are you doing with a dog in the Mall?" Quickly, I explained that Raven was a television star and I'd be glad to pick up her mess if he would bring me paper towels, etc. He looked down at the mess; he looked at me. "We'll clean it up," he said. "You can go." I think he smiled. There's an interesting postscript to this story. For the rest of Raven's career, she never had another potty accident.

Oh, I could go on.

Bloopers in front of a camera come in all shapes and sizes. One day I was walking on a sandy shore on an African lake, talking to the camera about fishing, when one leg sunk into the sand up to my thigh. Quick sand. It was not fun getting unstuck.

And we've had a few tippy canoes with expensive camera gear. Fortunately, nobody has been hurt and only one camera has taken a bath. That's not funny, either. That soaked video camera became a $35,000 piece of trash.

Raven is also a prolific blooper producer.

Time after time, I will deliver my lines to the camera with nary a stutter when she decides to yawn. Next, she looks totally bored.

Cut.

I resume my lines. She yawns again.

Cut.

How do you tell a dog not to yawn?

If you're wondering who's caused the most bloopers, well... that would be me. Saying dumb things, and stuff like that. Yes, we've also been lost, stranded and confused, too... Frankly, we've led an adventurous television life that, bloopers or not, probably isn't deserved.

But somebody (yawn) had to do it.

Cut.

In addition to Ron and Raven, here are some of the people who bring you Minnesota Bound's Emmy award-winning outdoor stories. Included are some **favorite moments, memories, personal interests** and background on their work with Minnesota Bound.

Aaron Achtenberg – PHOTO JOURNALIST / PRODUCER

What I Do At Minnesota Bound: Like everyone else here, I kind of do it all from shooting and editing stories, to on-lining shows and commercial production. But what really excites me is shooting and editing stories. Experiencing a new place and meeting new people is definitely one of the highlights of the job. It's a creative challenge and a lot of fun to bring the story you experienced in the field to life and make it interesting for the viewers.

Favorite Ron Moment: One of my favorite Ron moments happened in Omaha, Nebraska at the National Pheasant Fest. Ron likes to razz me about being from North Dakota. The usual jokes, no plumbing, no electricity and everyone is related. Well, we were at the conventions and met a few people from my home state. As it turns out, one guy happened to be my Dad's boss from a long time ago, and another happened to be my wife's cousin. I'll never hear the end of it from Ron. I guess we are all related in North Dakota.

My Favorite Minnesota Bound Story: It was shot on a little trout stream near Red Wing, Minnesota. We met the President of Carlton College, a passionate fly fisherman. He fishes in a tie and teaches fly-casting to the students of Carleton College. We only spent a few hours shooting, but it turned into one of the best stories I've ever done.

I live in Ramsey, Minnesota with my wife LeAnn, son Christian, daughter Elise and a lab named Jack.

Tony Capecchi - WEBMASTER

What I Do At Minnesota Bound: I'm the Webmaster, which is a fancy way of saying I play around online all day. We launched an online store where people can order special Ron and Raven DVDs. We also do a lot of cool Web cams on our site. We had a live underwater Web cam at Underwater Adventures at the Mall of America and we had a camera in the kennel of Raven's puppies. I consider it my personal duty to watch the Web cams multiple times throughout the day just to make sure everything's working right.

Favorite Minnesota Bound Story: My favorite story was Slick Deer Camp. It's truly an inspirational story, and Bill Sherck was good enough to give me a copy of the script to study for my own writing.

Favorite Ron Moment: When I was an intern Ron had me take Raven outside to relieve herself. The star of the show doesn't wear a leash, so she's got free roam. I remember thinking, "If anything happens to Raven, I'm never working another day at Minnesota Bound in my life!" Another favorite is as an intern I was helping set up for a shoot at a local park and a couple people came by to say hi to Ron. "This is Tony, our outstanding intern," Ron graciously said. "Out, standing on the sidewalk."

Little Known Fact: When I was a kid, Ron signed a T-shirt for me at one of his Kids Fishing Clinics. I always admired him so I saved it – it's in my closet and is still in decent shape.

Mike Cashman - PRODUCER/PHOTOJOURNALIST

What I Do At Minnesota Bound: I produce, videotape, and edit stories for our various shows. The best part of my job is being able to meet so many interesting, fun people who all have a story to tell.

Favorite Outdoor Activities: I like to fish, canoe, shoot pool, hike and bike, and I am a sports and horse racing fan.

Favorite Minnesota Bound Story: One of my favorite stories was a story I did on Ed Barcell, and

Floyd Doty, 2 fishermen who were both over 100 years old. We were able to get them both in the same boat together for an afternoon of fishing. It was great to see their love of fishing and life. My trip to Argentina and Chile was also a memorable fishing trip. The scenery was spectacular, and Ron caught a lot of fish.

Favorite Ron & Raven Moment: Was during a turkey hunting trip to the Florida Swamps. We had been hunting all day in the hot sun, and hadn't seen a single turkey. Finally a flock of seven turkeys came strutting down the road we were set up next to. They came within perfect range for Ron to harvest one, but he never shot. They left but then came back twice more and still Ron didn't shoot...he had slept through the whole episode and couldn't believe what had happened. True to Ron's good nature though we still did a story, only this one was on how he slept through his Florida Turkey hunt.

One Thing I Have Learned in Life: Forget the past. Live for today and think about the future.

Jared Christie - PRODUCER

What I Do At Minnesota Bound: Well, a little bit of everything you could say. I am a Producer/Reporter and I write and report for Minnesota Bound. It's great because one day I'll be in South Dakota on a pheasant hunt and the next day fishing for walleye. The rest of time I'm in the office setting up new stories or writing stories for upcoming shows. It's different every day.

Most Memorable Minnesota Bound Trips: There's so… many. Ok, I'll stick with two. Covering the Baja 1000. This was a 1,000 mile ATV race down the Baja Peninsula in 24 hours. It was just insane. A close second on my list would have to be a trip to Alaska. We spent a week camping, hiking and fishing from Anchorage to Seward. If you've never been, I'd advise you to start making plans immediately.

Favorite Ron Moment: I'd have to say my favorite Ron moment is usually around the holidays. We typically have a small Christmas party at the office where Joe brings the harmonica and Ron sings Kansas City, Kansas City here I come. It never gets old.

Favorite Outdoor Activities: Snowboarding, golf, running, biking and spending time with my dog Madi.

Interesting Fact: I recently moved back to Minnesota for the second time. My friends in California think I'm never coming home. I'm originally from California and attended San Diego State University, Go Aztecs!

Nicholas Clausen – VIDEOGRAPHER/EDITOR/PRODUCER

What I Do At Minnesota Bound: I work as a videographer, editor and producer at Minnesota Bound.

How it all Began: I have been an aspiring videographer ever since 9th grade when I produced the Friday Video Show at Central High School in St. Paul, Minnesota. After that, I went to college at Southern Illinois University at Carbondale where I received a B.A. in Radio-Television. I have also been a finalist for the National Press Photographers Association Photographer of the Year and been part of the team that won four regional Emmys.

Favorite Outdoor Activities: When I'm not begging my wife Laura to go camping, I'm whitewater kayaking, rock climbing, mountaineering, or ice climbing. I also love to throw the tennis ball around with our dog Ellie.

Favorite Minnesota Bound Stories: Probably my MOST favorite story was when Bill Sherck and I went to Alaska. There we gallivanted with the Kodiak bears, caught silver salmon, and summited the Talkeetna Mountain Range. My next favorite story would be a trip Ron and I took to the Outer Banks of North Carolina. There, we caught yellow fin tuna and striped bass. Our guide, Captain Tim Barefoot gave us a first class tour where we observed humpback whales and dined on some of the best seafood I've ever had!

Favorite Ron Moment: Ron was shooting a standup for a story we were doing on Stearns. He put on an inflatable life jacket and as he pulled the cord and the jacket squeezed around his neck, I saw his eyes grow to the size of golf balls. I think it startled him a bit, and we all had a good laugh. It's also good to see he's still enthusiastic after all these years of catching fish, it's still like he's catching the very first one.

Joe Harewicz – SENIOR PRODUCER

Words of Wisdom About Being a Producer: If you compare producing to baking a birthday cake, the producer gathers flour, eggs, yeast, ensures the oven is at the right temp, gets the birthday candles, makes sure the frosting is right and the details are right. If folks love the cake, great because with a weekly show, its time to bake another.

What I Do At Minnesota Bound: I wear many hats, I produce and write, but also shoot and edit. I love the variety. Viewers may find it surprising that often we distill hours, even days in the field into 4 or 5 "watchable" minutes. While the solitude and the slow pace of nature draws people outdoors, sometimes that doesn't translate to compelling TV. As Ron often reminds us – tell great stories.

Favorite Minnesota Bound Story: One of the first stories Ron and I worked on was about romance in the outdoors. In the middle of January, we trudged up the north shore in search of couples who embrace the outdoors. Deep in the back country, north of Lutsen, we hiked upon some winter campers. Ron tapped on a tent flap, the folks inside unzipped and said, "Wow! Ron Schara is at our camp site, will you please join us for some stew, and oh by the way, where's Raven?" Folks are quick to embrace his folksy charm and Raven. The original Raven was one of a kind. Smart and plenty cute too. When she saw me and the camera, she knew it was TV time. I think she liked the attention.

The People You Meet: In the course of producing 400 plus shows, I've been blessed to have met some interesting people. Folks who love the outdoor lifestyle and are passionate about it. I've noticed a trend, the folks who embrace the outdoors for the most part, have lots of energy, act younger than their years and are still curious and fascinated by the small wonder in nature.

Family Time: I have a wonderful 17 year-old daughter, a top student who loves the outdoors. I've shared time with her at Voyageurs National Park, the North Shore Superior Hiking Trail, floated the Zumbro River and explored many of Minnesota's great state parks.

Belinda Jensen – REPORTER

What I Do At Minnesota Bound: I am a features reporter for Minnesota Bound and get the opportunity to cover many different stories about the great outdoors. I am also the head meteorologist at KARE 11.

Best Time Fishing: I loved going fishing with my Dad, Uncle Rich, and my brother Jeremy on the Brule in Northern Wisconsin. I had been there so many times when I was a kid so it is fun to go back as an adult. We have caught some interesting fish...one we couldn't even name!

My Favorite Food: Pancakes and Milkduds.

People Would Be Surprised To Know: That I wish I could have been a great floral designer. I love flowers and plants.

My Favorite Book: I don't have time to read! Minnesota Bound, KARE-11, K102, Cities 97 and my son Tanner, my husband Dave, and my puppy Kula keep me so busy! I do try to read the paper everyday!

My Idea of a Relaxing Night: Would be cooking some new good recipes that I have ALL the ingredients for in the house and having a fire with my boys, David, Tanner & Kula!

Someday I'd Like To Try: I have tried a lot of things and some of them have been so crazy! So I would have to say...I would love to try to learn to sing! I am terrible but voice lessons would be fun.

Brian Maginnis – DIRECTOR OF SALES

What I Do At Minnesota Bound: I work with our advertising and sponsorship partners to maximize their exposure and sales to our millions of viewers and fans.

Favorite Ron Moment: Traveling with Ron and seeing all of the people who approach him and ask about Raven! It is remarkable and it happens coast to coast. It shows the power of television, but more so, the power of how Ron and Raven communicate and touch people. That is what makes our show stand out from the rest.

Favorite Saying: Luck is when preparation meets opportunity.

Interests: Fatherhood (Max), wingshooting, motorcycling, and home renovation.

Kelly Jo McDonnell – DIRECTOR OF OPERATIONS

What I Do At Minnesota Bound: It's my job to keep all the fires burning. I handle all the scheduling and organize the commercial traffic for the shows; research new locations and stories for the shows and I handle all contracts.

Favorite Minnesota Bound Stories: Of course, I loved the story on the Outdoor Women's weekend in Lanesboro, Minnesota. My Mother and I took part in that story. The feature done on the Okoboji, Iowa area and the Fishing Professor is also a favorite, since the Professor is my Father. Some other favorites are the feature we did on Bob Cary, the Hunt of a Lifetime and my absolute favorite show was the patriotic one we did after 9/11. It was spectacular.

Favorite Ron & Raven Moment: It's fun watching Ron & Raven off camera, especially the first Raven. She only had eyes for Ron. When she was in the office, and he'd leave to run an errand, she'd hover by the door and whine until he came back. She was never happy until he returned. Raven also likes to "beg" next to all of our desks in the office while we eat lunch. Raven has been known to pull a Subway sandwich right off of an editing desk.

Minnesota Bound Behind the Scenes: The funniest moments are when the guys take the "blooper" outtakes of Ron and loop them together on a tape that we show at our Christmas party every year. We get to watch Ron messing up lines, sinking into mud holes, falling asleep on camera while hunting, and answering his cell phone while turkey hunting. Ron and the guys really do have fun during their many trips, and that comes across "on" camera and "off."

Interests: Playing with my son Hayden, genealogy, and shooting hoops.

Steve Plummer - DIRECTOR OF PHOTOGRAPHY

What I Do At Minnesota Bound: I am the Director of Photography for Minnesota Bound. I joined Minnesota Bound in 1999 and since then have experienced some of nature's greatest gifts. While photography allows me to travel the world and meet unique people, my passion lies in putting the story together. I consider my "second life" in the edit bay as an opportunity to give viewers a chance to see and feel the story as I felt it. I have been honored in several areas over the years with 3 Emmy awards and 5 Emmy nominations.

How it all Began: I began my photojournalism career while attending school at the University of Wisconsin in Madison. I worked as a photographer and editor for a local Madison affiliate and later at Fox Television in Milwaukee.

Favorite Minnesota Bound Memories: Sleeping in a blind among tens of thousands of migrating Sandhill Cranes in Kearny, Nebraska. I also walked the glaciers of Alaska and filmed Kodiak bears from a stone's throw away. Closer to home, the Boundary Waters has brought fond memories of filming folks experiencing the Minnesota wilderness for the first time.

Favorite Minnesota Bound Characters: Two of my favorites include Scott Barton, a 13 year-old pheasant hunter who beat cancer and 79 year-old Otis W. Lael, a man with a lifetime of perspective and a love for making the most unusual hand-carved fish decoys.

I live in Vadnais Heights, Minnesota with my wife Kelly, our daughter, Bella, and our white German Shepherd, Greta.

Simone Schara – CONTROLLER

What I Do At Minnesota Bound: I wear many hats for Minnesota Bound. My main position is to take care of all finances. Other responsibilities include being the human resource contact to being the lady behind the leash when Ron is unable to appear with Raven. And there are many more hats beyond this list. An interesting behind the scenes fact – the office consists of 10 men and 2 women.

Favorite Ron and Raven Moment: It is amazing to see how many hearts Raven has touched. Another memorable moment was when Raven had the puppies because, I was privileged to keep one of her sons, Hoosier. He is my best friend and hunting buddy. As for Ron, I couldn't have asked for a better father. Another favorite moment, the famous appearance at the Mall of America when nature called for Raven – When you got to go! You got to go!

Minnesota Bound Favorites: My favorite part of the Minnesota Bound web site is the merchandise. I think we have some wonderful products and think all would enjoy Ron Schara's Outdoor Information Calendars.

Favorite Minnesota Bound Story: My Favorite has to be Bone Fishing in Bahamas.

I enjoy spending time with my son, Jake Ronald and our pets which include 2 dogs, Hoosier and Remy, 1 cat, Simpson and 2 horses, Ruby and DC.

Bill Sherck "Man About the Woods"
– WRITER & REPORTER

What I Do At Minnesota Bound: I write and report as part of Ron's crew. I got my television start along Lake Superior's Wilderness North Shore reporting local news and over the next decade worked as a field reporter for various ABC affiliates around the country and eventually Fox News. In 2002, I left news behind to pursue my real passion, the natural world. I was also part of the Minnesota Bound team that won the 2004 Emmy for writing.

Most Memorable Trips: My most memorable trips seem to be those that take us to the nooks and crannies of the world: Wallace, Idaho; Xcalak, Mexico; Elliott Lake, Ontario; Saltery Cove, Alaska and often, half the fun is getting there!

Favorite Ron Moment: Soon after I started with Ron, I hoped to prove to "the boss" that I was a competent fisherman. I set off to Gull Lake up in Brainerd to try and catch a couple of trophy pike. Turns out, I was able to hook a 40 and 42 incher that weekend. Like a proud son, I ran back to Ron with a couple pictures of the monster catch and release. Ron took a gander at the two snapshots, looked at me for a moment, glanced back at the pictures, then paused and said with a grave look, "A little advice for you…Don't outfish the boss." I smiled as Ron turned and started out the door. I'm guessing he chuckled a bit too.

Interesting Fact: I'm originally from Canada and an Eagle Scout.

Don Stremski - PRODUCER

How it all Began: My love of video began with a class at the local public access cable station in sixth grade. I majored in Photography at the College of Visual Arts in St. Paul, and have a degree in Television Production from Brown College. I think I can trace my inspiration to learn the technical aspects of television to when a test pattern interrupted a Gilligan's Island re-run when I was three or four, prompting me to wonder just what, exactly, they were "doing" down at the TV station, and how I could fix whatever it was that had gone wrong.

What I Do At Minnesota Bound: I provide technical support as well as Closed Captioning for the show each week. I am the last one to see and hear the program each week before it leaves the studio, and I prepare it for distribution to our various Network affiliates. I also work on special projects such as compiling video stills from the program archives for this book.

Favorite Ron & Raven Moment: One day, after spending the day shooting on Lake Minnetonka, Ron piloted the boat towards a swanky lakeside watering hole for a bite to eat. As he and Raven walked up the dock towards the restaurant, a bevy of attractive girls in bikinis came squealing towards him. "Look, it's Raven, the dog from TV!" they exclaimed, as they all stopped to pet the dog. "Oh, and Ron too. Nice doggy!" Raven loved it.

Raven "The Star" of Minnesota Bound

All About Raven.

To date, the Minnesota Bound television show has had only two stars of the show; with a third waiting in the wings. The original Raven was the first star until she died in October, 2005, at the age of 12. Her daughter, Rio, who was born July 15, 1998, was crowned the new Raven and also became an instant hit with viewers when she piloted a Crestliner pontoon, turning right while I shouted to turn left.

When it comes to conservation achievements, both Ravens really have been stars for the Pheasants Forever organization. The two dogs have helped Pheasants Forever acquire two public wildlife areas in Minnesota by raising nearly $1 million dollars.

When the original Raven became pregnant in 1998, I met with Joe Duggan of Pheasants Forever, along with John Remes, general manager of KARE-TV. We created a television campaign to raise donations to acquire wildlife land. It went like this: I knew the Raven puppies would be highly sought-after. So, we gave all viewers a free chance to sign up to adopt one of Raven's puppies. In return, viewers could voluntarily make a contribution to Raven's Prairie Heritage Fund.

The campaign's success surprised everybody. More than 6,000 people signed up to adopt the puppy. And they donated more than $25,000 to Raven's Fund.

Next, the folks at Gander Mountain stores volunteered to give $5 for every plush Raven puppy sold at their stores. They sold 10,000 plush pups and wrote a check to Pheasants Forever for $50,000. Pheasants Forever matched Raven's dollars twice, resulting in more than $250,000 for a wildlife land acquisition. A year later, Raven and I were invited to the dedication ceremony for a new 700-acre Two Rivers Wildlife Area in southern Minnesota, which had been acquired with help from Raven's fund. Oh, by the way, the puppy adoption was won by a pheasant hunter, Skip Hall, of St. Louis Park. He named his puppy, Easy. But winning the puppy out of 6,000 entries was anything but "easy."

In 2005, Raven and Pheasants Forever launched a new fundraiser, Help Raven Build A Wildlife Area. Again with help from KARE-TV, the Star Tribune, WCCO-Radio, Howard Tripp Agency and Mark Baker of Gander Mountain stores, we distributed thousands of plush Raven puppies, complete with their own bandana. For a $20 donation, folks could take home a Raven puppy and also help Build A Wildlife Area. In the first six months, $175,000 worth of puppies had been sold. When the campaign is complete, when all of the plush

Raven Facts

BORN: July 15, 1998

WEIGHT: 69 Pounds

MOTHERHOOD: Yes

VETS: Dr. Norb And Dr. Jay Epping, Blaine Area Hospital

REGISTERED NAME: Raven's Rum Rio

HER FATHER: Blackbird's Southland Moon

HER MOTHER: Rum River's Black Raven

FAVORITE FOOD: Eukanuba

FAVORITE TREAT: Eukanuba "Healthy Extras"

RESTRICTED FOOD: No table scraps or meat bones

BARKING: Seldom

BAD HABITS: None

SLEEPS: Outside in summer; inside in winter

SLEEPS WHERE: Not in Ron's bed!

FAVORITE GAMES: Catching frisbees or hunting Ringneck Pheasants

LIKES: To be petted by women

MORE LIKES: To ride in her Crestliner Pontoon

DISLIKES: Other dogs in her yard

puppies are sold, Raven will help raise close to $400,000 for Pheasants Forever's Help Build A Wildlife Area program. Hopefully, the $400,000 also will be matched twice by federal and state grants, reaching more than $1 million. All generated by the "Star of the Show."

Life With Raven

The most common question from viewers about Raven goes like this: How do you make her sit so still? The answer is training, of course. We started training Raven to sit in a kitchen chair while we ate. If she got down before being told to get down, she was scolded and placed back in the chair. She finally got it. But then something else happened. When the red bandana goes on (her TV costume), Raven began to add up 2 plus 2. She began to sit, heel or hop in her chair when wearing the red bandana. Dogs learn by association. Obviously, Raven learned that when the red bandana goes on, she must heel or otherwise be cool and sit still.

Now, if I had a shotgun or Frisbee in my hand, you would see a totally different Raven, a dog that can barely sit still from excitement and anticipation of fetching something. Remember, Raven is a retriever at heart.

As Raven gets older, we have allowed her to become more of a house dog, especially in the winter, although I still think outdoors is the best place. Labs are well–equipped for winter survival. But...well, Raven is a star.

In the yard, Raven is controlled by habit and by Invisible Fencing.

She rarely roams and is rarely allowed to roam. Fortunately, there are many things in our backyard for a Lab to sniff. Raven is a frog hunter, although I try to discourage the practice. She is forever pouncing in the tall grass in search of leaping frogs who usually get away. But not always.

Speaking of tall grass, Raven has been taught from puppyhood to head for the tall grass to go potty. In fact, that is my command, "Go Potty." This is a very practical habit to teach your dog and it helps keep your yard spot free.

Many folks wonder: Is Raven really your dog?

Obviously, the answer is yes. But don't take my word for it. Watch us on television or on stage.

Where I go Raven goes.
And where Raven goes, I'd better go, too.

Okay, now it's your turn to explore Minnesota and beyond. As you page through the stories in this book, you'll see a special Field Trip icon. This means we think this is an adventure for you, dear reader, that's worth taking. Consider the Field Trip icon as your invitation to follow in our footsteps. We promise you won't be disappointed (although it could rain a little.)

If you take one of our Field Trips, we'd like to hear how it went. Send us an email (fieldtrip@mnbound.com) about your adventure. The best stories will appear on our website, www.mnbound.

Definition: A field trip is a journey by people to a place away from their normal environment.

Field Trip Location

MAGICAL PLACES

MEMORABLE MOMENTS

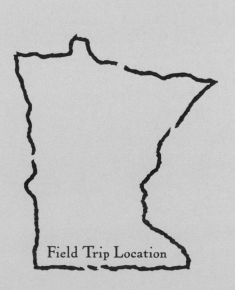

Field Trip Location

A Visit to the Agassiz Refuge

AGASSIZ NATIONAL WILDLIFE REFUGE, MIDDLE RIVER, MINNESOTA

America has made some smart choices over the last century, including the preservation of hundreds of national wildlife refuges. We tend to take these garden spots for granted. Why? I don't know. Maybe we haven't discovered their treasures. All of which explains why, on the 100th birthday of the nation's refuge system, we set out to explore a few national refuges in remote places. This is one of the stories.

Ron's Narrative: Mornings in America once began like this. And in some places they still do. This is Agassiz National Wildlife Refuge in Northwest Minnesota. A century ago, President Teddy Roosevelt signed into law establishing the nation's national wildlife refuge system. There are 540 of 'em now...540 gifts to ourselves, Charles Kuralt once said.

Maggie Anderson, Refuge Manager: Oh the wildlife at Agassiz is just phenomenal. We have over 280 species that can be seen, not only a large number of species but a large number of individual birds.

But refuges like Agassiz, the site of glacial lake Agassiz millions of years ago, don't just happen.

Gary Huschle, Refuge Worker: Agassiz is a very highly managed area. In the 61,500 acres we have 125 miles of roads, trails and dykes. We also have 20 managed pools with many controlled water structures. So, it's a refuge with a lot of infrastructure and it takes a lot of maintenance to keep it working, but without it this wouldn't be the place that you see.

On this morning, Gary Huschle, of the fish and wildlife service, is managing the life blood of the refuge, its water.

Gary: We want to coordinate the timing that it goes dry and turns into a mud flat with the shorebird migration… and provide them with good migration habitat.

A century ago the local folks thought this was good farmland and for 20 years tried to drain it.

Gary: They weren't able to pay their drainage ditch taxes to the county. In 1937 the Fish and Wildlife Service said we'll take the land from you and make it into a National Wildlife Refuge.

Now this farm raises wildlife.

Maggie: Out on Agassiz pool which is the largest pool in the refuge – Franklin Gulls are nesting. We have the largest nesting colony of Franklin Gulls in America and that varies from 15-25 thousand pairs. America needs these and we need to take care of them as well. Pressures are only going to increase – that's a given with our society, so we need to be sure that we don't lose what we have and we should improve upon what we do have.

So the day ends at Agassiz, doing just that, preserving what we have or even making it better. Better for the vast number of residents who live here.

Maggie: These are special places and my wish is that more people would visit them and realize what a special gift we have for ourselves.

Field Trip Location

A century ago the **local folks** thought this was good farmland and for 20 years tried to **drain it**.

A Visit to Alaska's Kenai
SEWARD, ALASKA

If you're looking for one of the most spectacular drives in America, here's a suggestion. Take the highway from Anchorage, Alaska to the small town of Seward, Alaska. It's guaranteed to please...unless you're expecting sand dunes and camel trains. We went to Seward looking for fishing adventure. We found the fish. And a whole lot more.

Ron's Narrative: So this is Seward's folly, huh? Alaska. Bought from the Russians in 1867. Price tag, $7 million. And this is downtown Seward, Alaska. Named after William H. Seward, the man ridiculed more than a century ago for spending $7 million of our tax dollars on land that couldn't be plowed.

Oh Billy Seward, you gotta be laughin' somewhere. Your folly has turned out to be priceless. Today, we'd pay $7 million for one mountain top.

Seward also got a good deal with the town that bears his name. Seward has more fishing boats than stoplights. The town is located on Alaska's Kenai Peninsula. It's a land rich with salmon rivers and calving glaciers.

Ron Schara: See the salmon jumping.

On this day the silver salmon, also known as Coho, are running in the pacific on the outskirts of Seward. And Neil Marlow, captain of The Shearwater, knows not only how to find 'em but how to catch 'em.

Captain Neil Marlow: Slide the hook through so that it puts the herring into a slight bend and then when you are mooching – you're just lifting up and down really slow – and that gives it a nice roll in the water.

Ron: This technique is called mooching, huh?

Neil: The most common mistake – the way we lose the most silvers is that you set the hook and nothing is there... You just want to keep reeling. A lot of times after they hit, they are coming up with it.

Soon we all were into jumping salmon. Some we caught. And some we didn't. No matter. When salmon bite in Alaska, they bite.

Neil: The silvers are a hatchery enhanced fishery. They return in the millions to Resurrection Bay. The limit is six fish per person, per day and a lot of the locals look at it like a harvest. It's their way to put away a winter supply of meat.

Ron: Come on silver salmon.

Neil: He's a beauty. A couple weeks from now this fish would be entering the fresh water streams to spawn.

Not just a few fish. Thousands.

Neil: Oh look over there. Salmon jumping everywhere here. Ooooh, my.

You say ooohh a lot when your fishing in Alaska. We discovered this the next day when Captain Marlow guided The Shearwater in search of other types of Alaskan fishing heavyweights.

Neil: We are going to jig for some Ling cod and some halibut. We'll fish with a lead head jig with a salmon belly for bait.

As young Alaskan natives, Neil and his sister, Leanne, have adopted the Kenai Peninsula as their home. Leanne is a school teacher who in the summer tourist season runs The Seward House, a bed and breakfast.

Leanne: I knew that when I wanted to settle in and find a place to teach and to live and do the lodging – it had to be near the ocean and Seward is a tight knit community.

Neil's chosen career: Fishing Guide.

Neil: This will be my 16th season. I started right out of high school as a way to pay for college and it developed as my career.

Ron: This is quite a contraption here on the end of my line. It's the biggest jig I've ever used. Fish on...

Neil: Looks like a giant pumpkin...Delicious...Cool.

If this is Seward's folly, we need more government programs just like it. Mountain vistas galore and plenty of tight fishing line.

Neil: One thing about fishing on the ocean bottom. You never know what you've got! It's a little bigger than the other.

Ron: Oh my goodness sakes what have I got?

Neil: A big Ling cod. That's a Ling cod. These Ling will eat whatever you put in their mouth.

Ron: Good fish... Heaviest I've had on today.

Neil: Boy they look like a monster coming out of there.

Did somebody say weird fish?

Neil: That's a China rockfish.

Ron: Yikes.

The China rockfish is also known as a Greenling. More of Seward's folly, no doubt. It seems no matter where you look on Alaska's Kenai Peninsula, you find wonder. As Captain Neil Marlow guided The Shearwater deeper into Cook Inlet, we found, well, more wonder.

A giant glacier stood before us. Chunks of blue ice slowly falling into the ocean. And you could hear kabloosh!

Ron: How can we be so mesmerized by a chunk of ice?

Neil: It is beautiful.

Ron: Hard to comprehend.

It is called the Colgate Glacier. As the ice fell, we were struck by the time warp. The ice falling into the ocean was probably a million years old.

Ron: It's like thunder, wow. A million years just fell into the ocean...

We picked up a chunk out of the salty sea. It might be old ice but it was still tasty. Mmm great water... Formed a million years ago.

Glacial ice might taste great but the most famous water on Alaska's Kenai Peninsula flows in the form of a river hell-bent for the sea.

This is the Kenai River.

Kenai Guide: How fast is this river going – 7 knots?

Probably since the day William Seward bought his folly, the Kenai River has drawn anglers to its swift waters. And for one big reason.

The Kenai is home to Alaska's supersized King salmon.

Hobo Jim: We have the biggest King salmon in the world – this river averages 43 pounds and they get up to 98 pounds.

Meet Hobo Jim. On a river full of Alaskan characters, he might be second to none.

Hobo Jim: When I was a kid, I hitchhiked and rode freight trains around the country and ended up in Alaska. I was real young but I stayed here. My last name is Varsos but most people just know me as Hobo Jim. Even my mom and dad call me Hobo Jim.

Hobo Jim has two passions in life. One of 'em is fishing the Kenai.

Hobo Jim: I fish this Kenai River almost every single day from May to October. It's the most incredible river in the world. We have 4 species of salmon and 2 runs of each.

Hobo Jim's other passion is strumming his guitar and singing his Alaskan songs.

Hobo Jim: When I was a kid, I was a commercial fisherman and a logger and I just started writing songs about things I was doing. Pretty soon people wanted to see me singing them instead of working.

And so he did. Hobo Jim's been singing and pickin' for more than two decades now. In Alaska, his CD plays right alongside the Rolling Stones and Alan Jackson. In fact, Hobo Jim is Alaska's official balladeer as voted by the state legislature and signed into law by the governor.

Ron: Is it easier to fish or sing?

Hobo Jim: I couldn't sing anymore without fishing first (laughter).

On the kenai, folks tend to keep their priorities straight.

A Visit to Hawk Ridge
DULUTH, MINNESOTA

With so many lakes, rivers and forests, Minnesota is a fertile land
for bird watching. But one of the most famous bird watching places
in the state is located high on a ridge overlooking Lake Superior and
the city of Duluth. As the wind blows and the thermals rise, you
don't find the birds, they find you.

Ron's Narrative: Every autumn it happens. Nature's own aerial show.

Hawk Watcher: This is a technique called scanning.

And our eyes turn to the sky.

Birder: You're just panning the sky. Osprey! In the blue into the white cloud.

The busy airway is full of migrating birds of prey.

Hawk Expert: This is a major flyway – an important part of the ecology of this area.

The flyway south also happens to follow the shores of Lake Superior

Hawk Expert: They get lift by thermals, hot air rising or heat rising off the earth
and then by updrafts from wind. Just like the wind over an airplane.

Any given fall day, they pass on high like tiny
airplanes. Hawks, eagles, osprey, even rare
peregrine falcons.

Hawk Watcher: Oh, overhead 1-2-3-4-5 birds,
pretty straight up.

A bluff just above Duluth provides the perfect
spot to spot the passing parade. It's now a 115
acre preserve aptly named Hawk Ridge.

Hawk Watcher: The expertise here is awesome.
People can ID a bird at, what is that? Half a mile?

While the bird watchers come and go, one of the hawk spotters seldom leaves his perch.

Dave Carman: 7:30 a.m. to 5:00 p.m. every day. Seven days a week!

Dave Carman works at Hawk Ridge – 70 hours a week, sixteen weeks straight. His job? To count the birds.

Dave: It's not work. To watch this, it's not work, it's a pure joy.

But Carman's bird count also serves a purpose. It's important to know bird population trends and who's who in the sky.

Dave: This is an immature sharp-shinned hawk.

Some birds also are captured and banded. And for a reason.

Dave: Nobody knew sharp-shinned hawks from the forests of Minnesota go all the way to Central America to go to Honduras and Costa Rica. Now we know because of banding from this site.

Such information, Carmen says, helps protect the habitat of these birds. And one more thing. It keeps the Hawk Ridge air show flying.

Dave: Oh, that is awesome! You'll hear over the course of a day the oohs and the ahhs. That's cool. That's really cool.

Cool...with an eye peeled to the sky.

Field Trip Location

You don't find the birds, they find you.

A Visit to Isle Royale
ISLE ROYALE, MICHIGAN

Somebody made a geological mistake a long time ago. When the map makers drew up Lake Superior, they assigned the lake's largest island to Michigan, of all places. How can that be? Isle Royale is closer to Minnesota than any other state. Michigan has football teams; why can't Minnesota have the island?

What's so fascinating about Isle Royale? Where do I start? How about fog and Lake Superior? How about wolves and moose? How about a chunk of earth largely unaltered by time? That's Isle Royale and that's why we went there.

Ron's Narrative: It's the largest island in the world's largest body of freshwater. Isle Royale, it's called.

A work of nature dating back 11,000 years. And oddly, it's an island larger today than a few thousand years ago. Isle Royale has long been an oasis of mystery and intrigue, its surrounding waters rich with fish; its rocky outcrops harboring potential riches, such as copper. For nearly 70 years, the island has been under the care of the National Park Service. Visitors today come to hike the island's many trails, to camp on its scenic vistas and explore a natural world largely isolated from Minnesota's north shore by 20 miles of water.

Island Visitor: I just love it. I just love it.

Even the waters around Isle Royale hold mystery as more than one ship met its match on the island's rocks. Yet, the island has become more than a park. It's a giant living laboratory that tests the ever-changing balance of nature. The main players in this drama are wolves and moose, whose fortunes go up and down in an endless drama about the relationships of predators and prey.

That's our Isle Royale story. A story that took 11,000 years to tell. Those who seek tranquility in this wilderness park are seldom disappointed. But travel far off the island's edge and you'll find a spot where even solitude gets lonely. It's a place of mystery...and of legend. It's a two hundred foot stone...called the "Rock of Ages."

The rock's only inhabitant is this lonely giant lighthouse. It was built in 1907, after two ships sank off a nearby reef. The Rock of Ages light created a beacon for the lost... and jobs for a few hardy souls, who from April to December, called it home.

Fifty one years ago a young coast guard man named John Tregembo got a new assignment.

John Tregembo: In the lighthouse service if a guy feels sorry for himself he's going to be lonely. Every morning when you turned off the light you had to come up here and put the shades on then you'd sweep the deck all the way down. Then if you got bad weather and had to start up the foghorn you had to come back up and take the shades off and go down and turn the light on and that's the way you lived.

Superior's pounding waves kept the job lively. And to get off the rock, well, the job was even livelier. One man would be running a 25 foot boat. He'd come in here, throw the boat in reverse, hook onto the main up there and it would lift you out of the water.

For Tregembo and four others stationed here, life was measured by weeks.

John: The time spent here was 21 days on the lighthouse then 7 days on shore.

The lighthouse stands 130 feet tall and in days gone by, this fancy French lens cast a powerful beam through the darkness.

John: In 1933 the passenger ship "George M. Cox" hit the reef in heavy fog. The lighthouse keeper carried out the largest mass rescue in Lake Superior history and had 121 guests for the day.

The keepers nowadays are of a different feather. Automated in the 1970's, Rock of Ages seldom sees visitors and its once proud light shows signs of a hard life. To John Tregembo it's like watching an ailing companion.

John: If I ever hit the lottery I'd see about making a bed and breakfast out of this. Then people could see what it was like to live in a real lighthouse.

But for now she stands alone with only the parting words of an old friend.

John: The two best lighthouses in the world are the one you're coming from and the one you're going to.

Of such are the tales from Isle Royale.

Superior's pounding waves kept the
job lively. And to get off the rock,
   well, the job was even livelier. One man
would be running a 25 foot boat.
   He'd come in here, throw the boat
in reverse, hook onto the main up there
   and it would lift you out of the water.

A Visit to Lake Bronson

BRONSON STATE PARK, LAKE BRONSON, MINNESOTA

While Minnesota attracts its share of tourists, summer or winter, there are some places that we tend to overlook. One of those is a nifty state park in the northwest corner of the state. We did this story to show folks what they've been missing.

Ron's Narrative: If parks are supposed to be for people, this may be the loneliest park in Minnesota. It's called Bronson State Park. Wild critters know where it is. Most Minnesotans do not.

Ken Anderson, Park Manager: It's a little different. We have one of the more significant prairie resources in the state. Which is something that there's not a lot left of. I believe it's only like 1 or 2 percent of the prairie that was originally found in Minnesota is still surviving. So we're working to change that.

The lake that Lake Bronson State Park is named after was created during the depression in the 1930's as a result of the drought. The result in 1937 was the creation of a state park in Minnesota's extreme northwest corner. It's a long ways from just about everything except mother nature.

Ken: In the summertime, I enjoy just watching, taking a walk out through the prairie areas, and through the big blue stem grasses that are 6, 7 feet tall. The Pasque flower is the first flower to come up in the spring. Sometimes it will even come up in the snow. They are delicate and can only be found in the prairie.

Bronson State Park also reflects a chapter from American history, the days of WPA's public works programs.

Ken: Well, some of the more significant ones, more obvious to park visitors, are the observation tower, which is unique. It was built as both a water tower and an observation tower. The dam itself was built in 1936.

There's another historical lesson in the park, marked by the presence of tombstones.

Ken: Actually there are two cemeteries. One only has two graves. For some of the early settlers, this was their home. They were buried here.

The rest of the park was created by nature.

Ken: We have the largest Jack Pine found in North America. It's a survivor. It shows the weather and the ravages of time.

While the park remains a long way from many people, busier times are ahead. Students from area high schools have discovered its natural classroom. And more lessons await inside the interpretative center. But there's still a good chance, Lake Bronson State Park – on any day – will have an empty bench surrounded by plenty of nature.

An empty bench, just waiting for you.

Field Trip Location

It's a survior. It shows the weather and ravages of time.

A Visit to Voyageurs National Park
VOYAGEURS NATIONAL PARK, INTERNATIONAL FALLS, MINNESOTA

Voyageurs
National Park

A great moment in Minnesota's history was the day, the U.S. Congress passed a measure creating Voyageur's National Park in northern Minnesota. The park's birth was controversial at times but eventually the idea of preserving such a unique resource became the right thing to do. I was actually one of the first to explore Voyageurs after congress created the Park. We did so on snowmobile. Today my favorite way to explore Voyageurs is by houseboat. And why not? Voyageurs was and is the nation's only National Park reachable only by water. And now, it is for evermore.

Field Trip Location

Ron's Narrative: To hook a smallmouth bass, to watch it jump and jump again, is a special moment in this pursuit we call fishing.

Woody, The Guide: Oh I got a nice smallie here on this toy rod and reel. Oh it don't get any better than that. Oh look at that – the size of that honey. Oh man that was a nice fish.

Now add an unforgettable sunset to the day's last casts.

And you realize you're a lucky dude. Lucky to be fishing in this place called Voyageurs.

Voyageurs National Park. Endless water and countless islands. Calling loons and hungry smallmouth.

It's America's only water bound National Park with miles of roadless wilderness. Where the only way to reach a walleye or cast a popper fly to a waiting bass is by boat. Fishing boat or houseboat.

Billy Dougherty, Rainy Lake Houseboats: It's the only wilderness lake that I know of that you can still drive to and put a boat in and still have a wilderness experience and it's undeveloped by man. The last road is where you launch your boat.

This is Rainy Lake, 70 miles long, and the largest of three major lakes in Voyageurs.

Barry Woods, Guide: We have a very diverse fishery – we have smallmouth and largemouth bass, crappies, muskie, sturgeon, northern pike and walleye.

Dave Lenz, Fly Angler: Oh, is that fun when you can watch 'em come up to the fly. This is why you come to Rainy Lake.

Like the joy of a good fish, a sense of history also lingers over this land. As the park's name implies, Voyageur explorers once paddled this way looking for furs and a watery route to the Pacific. The Voyageurs were followed in the 1800's by trappers and loggers who lived it up here at the Kettle Falls Hotel. It's said – a hardboiled woodsman could rent a room here and hire a lady for the night. Today, the ladies are gone but the hotel bar room remains open, though the bar room floor is a little bent out of shape.

Further on in Voyageurs, you'll find Lake Namakan. Like Rainy Lake next door, Namakan harbors smallmouth bass, golden walleye and plenty of camping sites for tents and houseboats.

Justin Ebel, Voyageur Houseboats: Tighten up my line and get it parked for the night. The key to tying up is to get the boat on shore level, don't run too fast and keep the lines nice and tight.

We were ready to rough it.

Justin: You got the radio and the stereo, the radio is a marine band, the stereo would be for the CD player which is next to the television.

Raven was ready too. Lake Namakan offered flying loons one minute and flopping fish the next. Does a Labrador need more? Did somebody say swimming moose? Time stands still where moose roam. The giant deer have survived the centuries in Voyageur National Park. Just like the aged granite. Just like Namakan's walleyes.

Our walleye pattern was pretty old fashioned, too, a jig and minnow.

Mike Lessard, Fishing Guide: There's plenty of fishing opportunities no matter which way the wind is blowing – it's blowing into the bays.

Wind and walleyes. It's a combo that keeps you coming back to Voyageurs.

Chef John Schumacher: Alright boys breakfast is served, come on, rock and roll.

Meet Chef John, The Game Gourmet. Chef John is a natural as an outdoor cook. While a houseboat breakfast with Chef John is a little different and very tasty. We discovered our guide for the day was a fella by the name of Leverne. He was a little different, too. Leverne's been roaming these parts for hire since he was 11 years old. Now at the age of 85, Leverne's still fishin' or wishin' he was.

Leverne Oveson, Fishing Guide: It's just fun fishing (laughter). I just like to fish. I get a kick out of getting a bite. I get as much kick as I did when I was a kid.

In many ways, Leverne is still a kid.

Leverne: What did you do in the old days to figure out how deep the water was? Well, I just fished. When my sinker hit the bottom I knew how deep it was.

One autumn day Leverne told me he's found more than good fishing out here in the land of the Voyageurs.

Leverne: Well, we had the old wood boats and no depth finders. We learned the lake by hitting the rocks which I did. I've hit 'em all I think a couple of times.

When he found the rocks, Leverne also found the walleyes.

Leverne: I've had a good life. If I should die tomorrow I'd die happy. It's been fun. I never worry about tomorrow up here. You do the best you can today.

No, it's not always Camelot here amid the granite and Red Pines. But somewhere in Voyageurs there's always a good time waiting. And when you find it, you wish those days wouldn't end.

A Visit to Whitewater State Park
WHITEWATER STATE PARK, ALTURA, MINNESOTA

I think we tend to take our state parks for granted. They're a place with tables for picnicking, huh? Yes, but more than that. Each park by definition is a special place in Minnesota. One of the jewels in the state's treasure chest. For that reason, every park is a story for us. Especially a place called Whitewater.

Ron's Narrative: The last glacier to slide into Minnesota a few eons ago flattened everything but this corner of the state. Today it's called bluff country.

Park Manager: I think any Minnesotan that has visited the bluff-lands realizes what a unique place it is. It's only 3 percent of Minnesota that looks like this.

Way back in 1919, Minnesotans decided to preserve a big chunk of these bluffs and valleys. It's called Whitewater State Park.

Park Manager: I think many Minnesotans dropped here in the middle of the Whitewater Valley if asked "Are you in Minnesota?" – would say no. It doesn't look like most of Minnesota. It is such a small area and yet it's an area so rich in life. In fact, Whitewater has more plants and animals – the richest biodiversity – of any landscape in Minnesota.

Visitors to Whitewater State Park also learn what's not here. It's some kind of Minnesota miracle.

Park Manager: There are no mosquitoes here. I have been here 27 years now and have yet to use insect repellent. That usually gets everybody's attention when you tell them about the mosquito shortage. If you see one or two or hear them buzzing in your ear, that's pretty unusual.

What's a trout angler to do with no bugs to swat?

Park Fisherman: I'm hoping to catch some rainbow or some brown trout. They stock rainbows in here – the brown tend to be more natural – they reproduce in this stream. It's just a really beautiful area – high bluffs and low valleys – the trout fishing is just incredible.

Incredible seems to be a good word to describe Whitewater. Including something called the Elba Tower. Back in the 1930's, the tower was used to spot forest fires. Today it's just part of exploring a park – all 132 steps.

Park Angler: It's just a beautiful area of the state. There's a lot of diversity, a lot of opportunity to do different things.

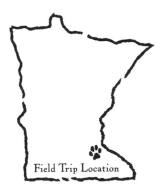

Field Trip Location

As state parks go, the Whitewater isn't easy to forget. All you have to remember is this park is where the trout bite, but the mosquitoes don't.

Boundary Waters Magic
BOUNDARY WATERS, MINNESOTA

The clearest way into the universe, John Muir wrote, is through a forest of wilderness. Maybe that's why so many of us come to this wilderness, known as the Boundary Waters Canoe Area Wilderness, the BWCAW, in northern Minnesota. Maybe we're looking for something. Something out there amid this roadless, million acre maze of waterways and islands.

Whatever it is, it must be something important. To get there, we lug packs and canoes over portages. Rain or shine, it doesn't matter. We seem driven to be there, paddling onward, each canoe stroke bringing us closer to some unknown prize.

Maybe it's our spirit we seek?

Wilderness author Sigurd Olson thought so. Without divorcement from outside influences, he wrote, man cannot know what spirit means. We seek it so intensely maybe that's why the BWCAW has such a history of turmoil. Some folks want more use of motors; others want less. Bob Cary just wants peace.

Bob Cary: I've never been mad at anybody in a motor boat. I've paddled all my life. Maybe I'm too old but I don't understand people being angry with somebody else because of the type of watercraft they're in. I'm more interested in how they camp and how they take care of the woods.

Ron's Narrative: None of us come to the wilderness to argue. It's a simpler lifestyle we seek where we can go one on one with bugs that bite. Somewhere along the way. We start to find what we're looking for.

Bob: There are not many places in the world where you can drink the water right out of the lake.

A wilderness trip can be humbling. When the canoe tips or the sleeping bag gets wet. But we learn from that, too.

A wilderness, John Muir said, is where nature may heal and give strength of body and soul alike.

"It's a place wrapped in granite stone.
And chained with clear blue waters.
Where glaciers marched and left a path
For the rest of us to follow.
Loons call in springtime.
And ravens ring in winter.
While sled dogs race atop the ice.
Where paddlers paddled last summer.
We each come here in search of self.
And answers to our questions.
We find them in the biting fish.
While sunsets ease our tension.
It's a magical place, the BWCAW.
As if nature was run by elves.
It may explain for the rest of time.
We must protect it from ourselves."

Field Trip Location

Post Script: My fishing friend Bob Cary has taken his final portage.

Ecuador Adventures
CUYA BENO RAIN FOREST, EASTERN ECUADOR

We all know...in life we only go through once. But I've also learned that once is not always enough. There's a lot of world out there to explore. So let us not dillydally. This may explain why producer Joe Harewicz and I took our TV cameras to Eastern Ecuador to one of the world's most remote rain forests. Considering our one time crack at life, why not? This trip will be remembered by me as a lifetime highlight. So many experiences, so many vivid memories.

Yet, in hindsight, the rain forest adventure was more risky than I realized at the time. Trouble was never far away. Did we survive? Of course. Sure, we had plenty of bug bites and bug encounters. We had days of downpours and long rides in swift rivers with remote shores. While our native guides were at home; we were always strangers in a very strange land. Would I go back? What day do you want to leave?

Ron's Narrative: Some mornings, long before your eyes open, the sounds that surround you announce you may be arriving in your own twilight zone. Look around. Nothing is ordinary. Not the trees, not your neighbors. They seem friendly enough. You only hope they are.

For a male weaver bird, a foggy dawn simply begins another day of courtship songs and basket weaving high in the treetops.

Me? I'm surrounded by thatched roofs, deep in the Cuya Beno Rain Forest of Eastern Ecuador.

Float this river far enough, the natives say, and you can paddle all the way to the Amazon. Unless, of course...Something gets you first. It doesn't take you long to realize. In this Ecuadorian Rain Forest, you're in another world and in another time from whence you started.

Our adventure began in Quito, which is Ecuador's capital city and, at 9,000 feet, one of the highest cities in the world. At such an altitude, the natives say, it's eternal springtime. Quito is alive in classic Latin American fashion. Bright music. Great art. Friendly faces.

A day later, we were a world away. And loading a freighter canoe to ride a jungle highway downstream, the Aguarico River. But downstream on the Aguarico also was a ride back into time itself.

Gere Pedersan: Sounds that you never heard before, smells that you never smelled before, sights that you never saw before, wonderful people. It's an adventure around every turn of the river.

Gere Pedersan, a Norweigan entrepreneur, has been down the Aguarico River before. He and his partner, Gere Aasgord lead nature tours into Ecuador's little known rain forest.

Gere Aasgord: This is a unique part of the world, there is so much to discover, the insects, the plants, and the animals and people, very different from Norway but I like it.

But reaching this land where time has stood still isn't easy. To help us, Gere befriended natives, members of the Keetchwah Tribe.

Gere A.: They are so relaxed...no stress, no relationship to a watch. If it's 9 or 11 o'clock it doesn't matter, they'll just walk around a little bit in the forest or hunt or fish a little bit.

Our stops at villages along the river provided a glimpse into Keetchwah life. Most of their food, even their pets, come from the wild.

Gere P.: Due to oil exploration, the world is coming here every day. Why should the Indians here not have mobile telephones, computers or TVs...today we have a boat with an engine. We eat food cooked by a generator. All these things are gradually being adapted by the Indians. It's good for them but not for the Indian culture, cuz little kids that you see around here grow up with these things, so it's not going to be trendy, to make things like dug out canoes. So their culture is dying, a vanishing tradition. You and I are among the last generation to see this, the next generation will see this in a museum, or on a TV show...maybe yours.

A cast into jungle backwaters is like no other. We paddle into watery haunts in search of Peacock bass. And we're not disappointed.

Ron Schara: There's a classic Peacock bass, male knob on his head and spot on his tail.

But, in truth, you never know what's about to bite back.

Gere A.: We have three piranhas, the red breasted, the white and the spotted. I guess the black is here too, but I've never seen it.

Ron: There is something really exciting about fishing in the jungle, cuz if you are like me raised on Tarzan movies, you come to expect in quiet water like this, something exciting is going to happen, every cast is an experience waiting to happen.

In the rain forest rivers of Ecuador, there are some 350 fish species to experience. One of them is called the Gwacka Mayo or Parrot catfish.

Gere A.: This catfish can be more than 100 pounds, sometimes more than 500 pounds. It's a giant.

To catch the Parrot catfish, our Parrot ploy was a gob of cut fish for bait. Gere, my catfish coach, clearly was an angler of catfish passion. The question is why?

Gere A.: I don't know... Ha ha ha. I'm nervous to lose it and to see it. Waiting and waiting, wondering what kind of a catfish is it, is it one I have never seen before, how big is it, is it a world record – you never know.

One foggy morning, our luck was about to change. I reared back on a jumping fishing pole and set the hook. But the big catfish swam around a sunken tree branch. Quick as a cat, Gere, my guide, jumped into the dark, chocolate jungle river water.

Ron: Can you feel the tree?

Gere P.: No, I feel a fish.

Gere A.: It feels like it's by a tree and rubbing on a tree.

Ron: This is a standoff – that's what it is. You're talking about a fish from 20 pounds to over 100 and this one is somewhere in between.

Quickly Gere realized the big cat was tangled in a tree snag.

Gere P.: Give me a little line.

Ron: Don't wrap the line around your hand in case the fish takes off. Oh there, oh there he is. He's huge.

It seemed like forever but at last the big cat was done.

Ron: Oh my goodness, I think he's ready to come in.

Gere A.: Oh my, that's a catfish!!! Isn't he gorgeous? So colorful. Now, you know why they call him the Parrot fish.

Ron: I can't stretch my fingers between his eye balls – and I suppose your going to tell me this is a small one.

Gere P.: It is a small one...(laughter). He is about 80 pounds – the world record is 97. I'm gonna let him grow up. Adios papa.

Ron: He's gone.

Paddling back into time might be easy to say. But it's not easy to do. A two day journey by freighter canoe has taken us deep into one of western Ecuador's last wilderness frontiers, the Cuya Beno Wildlife Refuge.

Our Norweigan travel guides, Gere Pedersan and Gere Aasgord, lead the way.

Gere A.: This is a tropical Rainforest. It holds the highest diversity of trees. It holds the world record of 472 species of trees found in one hectare. 472 different trees is crazy and the number of bird species is mind boggling.

Gere P.: Europe holds 6 or 7 hundred species and here in Ecuador it's like 1600.

Gere A.: When people ask me why are there so many species here, the question leads to a larger question because the tropics have always been the tropics. The birds and animals that live here have been here for millions and millions of years. So that's why there are so many species.

So many birds, so many parrots.

Gere P.: Parrots eat fruit, and as a defense for being eaten the fruit have venomous compounds, which can be lethal to the parrot. That is why every day the parrots fly to certain places along the river and eat sand which contains nutrients that break down the poison.

Our native guides were members of the Keetchwah tribe. Despite a language barrier, they were anxious to share their ancient ways of hunting and fishing.

One day in mere minutes, one guide, Maysayas, crafted an animal trap using only tree bark and branches.

Gere P.: The trap is used for catching birds and small rodents. They have done it for thousands of years. When they were young there was no communication here, just forest. It was hunting with blow guns with no support from the outside. They've learned how to use nature and the plants and animals for their way of living.

Gere A.: This is a plant used for snake bites when you crush the leaves. They also have plants to fix toothaches or to make tea for drinking.

For Messiah, a tribal elder, finding something to eat at any time, any place, wasn't a problem.

Messiah: Will you have one Ron? It's muy bueana.

Messiah showed me a large white grub. He said it would turn into a beatle. He said it also tastes good. Like coconut creme.

Messiah: It's good for the flu.

As it turned out, Messiah was right. It did taste like coconut, although I couldn't chew a whole grub. As a self taught naturalist, Messiah was eager to show us to more unique sights, including a parade of leaf cutter ants.

Gere P.: It's amazing to think that this is one of the oldest eco systems on the planet and untouched since dinosaurs roamed the earth, which is like 65 million years ago.

Not many fishing places are like the rain forest of eastern Ecuador. Strange sounds. Strange sights. And plenty of strange fish.

Ron: That is a good one. He hit that old spinner bait (ha ha ha). They remind me of a smallmouth bass; they have a lot of heart.

I was off to a fast start catching small peacock bass, a fish of the jungle. Which made me feel like the king of the jungle.

Ron: Another great Peacock bass. We got the bait now; we're gonna clean up.

Feeling smug, I challenged Messiah to a little fishing contest. My fancy fishing gear versus his handmade canoe, handmade spear and handmade bow and arrow.

Suddenly the fishing slowed. Mesiah was off to a poor start. But then, so was I. Suddenly....Messiah tossed his spear and bingo.

Ron: So how'd you do that Messiah?

Before I could say nice shot, Messiah had another fish. Me? I kept on casting. final score? Well, deep in a rain forest who really cares? Sure, Messiah probably was hungry, which may explain why he did so well. Me? I was just fishing for the fun of it.

The Magic of the North Shore
NORTH SHORE OF LAKE SUPERIOR, MINNESOTA

One of Minnesota's most popular tourist destinations is known as the North Shore of Lake Superior. There are many reasons why so many of us want to go there. The lake, of course. The interesting folks who live there. But there's something about the shore, itself, that beckons.

In a phrase, this is a fascinating piece of the earth. Folks who live nearby call it the North Shore. The North Shore of Lake Superior. It is rocky. It is rugged. It is historic in an earthly sense of the word.

The North Shore has existed for roughly a million years, give or take an era or two. When volcanoes belched and glaciers moved, they left behind a North Shore layered with lava rock and granite as old as any on the surface of the earth. But that's the stuff for rock hounds.

To others, the North Shore has a magnetism that doesn't fit into a glacial time warp. The world's largest sea of freshwater has its own mystique, rolling and pounding endlessly on the ancient rock.

Dozens of rivers tumble down the slope of the North Shore, falling a thousand feet or more to reach the big lake in a whitewater rush. Except in winter. During winter on the Gooseberry River, the spectacular Gooseberry Falls hangs frozen in time, reduced to a mere trickle on its way to the inland sea.

A popular man-made site along the North Shore is historic Split Rock Lighthouse. It stands 100 feet above superior on a solid rock cliff. From Duluth to Grand Portage, the North Shore runs as a rugged edge, creating an endless parade of scenic vistas that seem to tug at the heart.

That may explain why so many lovers seem to come here. Nobody knows exactly what inspires so many honeymoon trips to the North Shore. Maybe it's the lovers hope for longevity. May their love life be like the North Shore, as lasting as the granite and as breathless as the superior sea.

Nobody knows exactly what inspires so many honeymoon trips to the North Shore.

Field Trip Location

Mississippi Refuge
UPPER MISSISSIPPI NATIONAL WILDLIFE REFUGE

I have no witnesses, but there's a good chance the first fish I ever caught came from the Mississippi River. My folks spent many a Sunday afternoon sitting on the bank of the river's backwaters. We fished for bluegills, mostly. And even a kid my age knew when the bobber went down.

With such memories, the Mississippi River holds a special place in my heart. I also felt I owed a favor to the river for all of those fond boyhood times. When America celebrated a century of wildlife refuges, I knew the Upper Mississippi National Wildlife Refuge held a special place in refuge history. For me, telling this story was payback time for my beloved Mississippi.

Ron's Narrative: No matter how you see it...from the river...from the blufftops... from the sky – you see a ribbon of wild and unmatched splendor. From Wabasha, Minnesota to Rock Island, Illinois. Two hundred and sixty miles in length, touching four states and cradled in the valley of America's Father of Waters. This is the Upper Mississippi River National Wildlife Refuge.

Don Houltman, Refuge Manager: I call the Upper Miss one of the crown jewels of the refuge system – it's magnificent in all ways.

And in ways almost uncountable. Some 305 bird species – more than 130 bald eagle nests and roughly 134 different species of fish.

Don: So from diversity and the sheer numbers of birds that come here – It's the heart of the country as far as flyaways.

But perhaps the most incredible fact about the refuge is that it's here at all. River Rat and author, Ken Solway, lives and breathes the river's blood.

Ken Solway: It is a place amidst a corridor of human activity that is wild and free. We have a railroad on each side of the river; we have a major highway on each side of the river. We have airplanes that fly up and down the river. And yet the wildlife thrives. And it's a great lesson.

Don: It was one man and one group that really got it started and that was Will Dilg, who was one of the founding fathers of the refuge. He fell in love with the Mississippi. He was from Chicago, he fished here – he used the river, and always loved it.

Amazingly Congress agreed, establishing the Upper Mississippi Refuge in 1924. Soon after, federal workers began to restore the river valley's wildlife habitat.

Don: We have a staff of 42 full time people and we're divided into 4 districts. Today the Upper Miss is one of about 535 wildlife refuges in a national system launched in1903 by President Teddy Roosevelt.

An avid hunter and conservationist, Roosevelt's vision was to preserve wildlife for future generations.

Don: This is one of the most visited national wildlife refuges in the country, 3.5 million visitors a year come here.

Refuge worker, Bob Drieslien has seen it all.

Bob Drieslien: It's just a neat place and the river is such a tremendous migration pathway for birds during migration.

In the autumn, they come. Tundra swans – swans by the dozens. In the spring, they soar. Bald eagles – eagles by the dozens. Even rare Blanding's turtles survive here, despite dodging traffic to reach their traditional egg laying grounds. Ducks, too – sometimes 70 percent of the world's Canvasback duck population pause at the refuge during the fall migration.

Don: Our big challenge for the future is... how are we going to manage this resource so we keep what makes it so special now without loving it to death?

Bob: I'd like to see more effective water management. I think the key is being able to manipulate water levels in these pools and try to bring plants back. And it's going to be a real tough job.

Ken: The big problem I see is siltation. What happens is the great river is a reflection of its tributary and what happens to the tributaries (muddy streams that flow into the river) happens to the river.

Don: I hope I leave this refuge a better place. I tell the staff that all of us as we work at these refuges, we sort of leave a couple of bricks in the foundation and we build upon the work that's gone on before us. So we all help to leave it a better place.

Ken: What is good for the land is good for the people. It's a real simple thing

Yes, what is good for the country is good for the people. Teddy Roosevelt understood that. So did that fella Will Dilg who gave us the Upper Mississippi Refuge. Now it's ours. Ours to pass on.

Yes, what is good for the country is good for the people. Teddy Roosevelt understood that. So did that fella Will Dilg who gave us the Upper Mississippi Refuge. Now it's ours. Ours to pass on.

Wind Cave Adventure
WIND CAVE NATIONAL PARK IN HOT SPRINGS, SOUTH DAKOTA

I was a young kid fresh out of Iowa State University when I first came to the Black Hills of South Dakota. Part of my job as editor of South Dakota's Conservation Digest was to visit different parts of South Dakota and write stories about all the great things being done by the state's game and fish agency.

On that first visit, I saw the first elk of my life, first mountain goat, first mule deer and first wild turkey. Needless to say, the Black Hills became a magical place for me. And....it still is. There's a never ending parade of Ponderosa Pines in the hills, along with a never ending parade of nifty stories, including one of the longest caves in north America. One of our Videographers, Aaron Achtenberg, was sent to explore the place called, Wind Cave National Park.

It's located, you know where.

Ron's Narrative: When the wind blows in the Black Hills – blows beyond the famous faces, it is not always from east or west or north or south.

Here at Wind Cave National Park, the wind blows far beneath the earth.

Phyllis Cremonini, Park Ranger: We're going to the lower landing which is about 200 feet down into the assembly room. When visitors come to see Wind Cave they expect to see the more common formations such as stalactites and stalagmites they see in other caves throughout the country and throughout the world. Here at Wind Cave we don't have much of those formations.

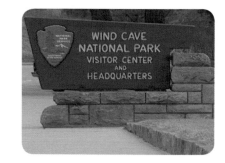

And there might not be a national park here if it wasn't for the whoosh of wind that attracted the attention of two hunters back in 1881. What Tom and Jesse Bingham found was an opening in the earth about two feet wide.

Phyllis: The story goes that one of the brothers leaned down to look into the hole and at the time there was a lot of air rushing out of the hole and his hat blew off. Then in probably about the late 1890's, we had some folks called the McDonalds come up and set up a homestead. Alvin McDonald, who was their 16 year old son, decided to do some exploring in the cave and he actually was our first true explorer. Alvin mapped out probably a good 9 or 10 miles of the cave's passageway.

In 1903, Wind Cave became the 7th national park in the nation, signed into law by President Teddy Roosevelt. Today Wind Cave abounds in scenic ponderosa and is home to a rich variety of wildlife, from elk to bison, from bluebirds to prairie dogs.

Phyllis: Wind Cave, the actual entrance itself is only about the size of a basketball. The wind or the air rushes in or out depending on the atmospheric pressure. When the pressure changes it'll either blow in or out. And it can be pretty significant. We've tested the air coming through the passageway and we've been able to test it up to 70 mph.

But visitors to the cave will discover more than a breeze.

Phyllis: It's this big 3-dimensional maze that we're gonna go into today. Which makes it the most complicated cave in the entire world. All 108 miles of the cave system are all actually under 1 square mile of surface area. What we're looking at right here is boxwork. It's a very rare cave formation found in very few places throughout the world. And about 95 percent of the world's boxwork is found here in Wind Cave.

Some of the other formations we have here in Wind Cave is called cave popcorn. It's the bumpy stuff you see here. That's formed when water is seeping out of the wall and leaving a calcite formation as the water is evaporated. Currently we've mapped out a little over 107 miles of passageway. We're now ranked as the 6th longest cave in the entire world.

...long and windy.

A Wonderful Conservation Story
BADLANDS, NORTH DAKOTA

America's hunters claim to be the first conservationists. It might be true, but it's also true that most Americans don't share the same opinion. Unaware of the wildlife contributions made by hunters, many people think wildlife would be better off without hunting. Every fall on the vast and lonely prairies of western North Dakota, in a place called the Badlands, you can see a wonderful conservation story. It's about the comeback of wild sheep. And you'll never guess whose making it happen.

Ron's Narrative: Slowly the sun peaks into North Dakota's Badlands. High on a hill, Pete, a wild sheep expert, peers through his binoculars and counts the big horns.

Pete Cimellaro, A Wild Sheep Expert: 1,2,3,4,5,6,7,8 of 'em.

Jimmy, a Hunter from Arizona, waits for Pete's directions.

Pete: Jimmy, we're going to go around to this other side until we get the wind in our face.

Jimmy Jamison: Sounds like a good plan.

It's chilly in the Badlands on this October morning. Badlands – the name fits. Two million acres of no man's country in western North Dakota, country carved by centuries of gully washers and relentless prairie winds. A century ago, an American president, the roughrider, Teddy Roosevelt, loved coming here to explore and to hunt.

In Roosevelt's time, wild Audubon sheep roamed the Badlands until disease and uncontrolled shooting early in the 1900's led to the animal's extinction. Now a century later, it looks like a scene from yesteryear. Hunters once more stalking the Badlands for wild sheep, a species known as rocky mountain bighorns.

Pete: The ram is just to the right of this knob. We're going to go right at this knob. Both rams are laying right over about 200 yards away.

Two majestic rams are bedded down and unaware. Unaware of the hunter's stalk. Unaware they are the subjects of one of America's great conservation success stories.

It's also a story about sheep hunters. Hunters stepping to the plate to save the bighorns of the Badlands.

Pete: Ok, Jimmy, ease your rifle up real slow.

Meet Jimmy Jamison, an Arizona hunter who doesn't let a bum leg keep him away from his passion. To be in the company of wild sheep. It's a passion shared by his guide, Pete Cimellaro.

Pete: Being with sheep is like a disease. I don't know how you catch it other than you just get it. It's a lifetime disease. We've got about 6,000 members of the Foundation for North American Wild Sheep and most of them have a case of sheep sickness. It's a situation where you love to hunt sheep, you love to watch sheep, and you love to look for sheep.

To a sheep hunter, a sheep hunt means long and hard hiking.

Jimmy: There's usually no such thing as an easy hunt.

As all sheep do, bighorns love high places. Although the towering walls and peaks of the Badlands may not be high by mountain standards, the bighorns seek safety in the baddest of the Badlands.

Randy Kreil: Currently we estimate we have about 200 bighorn sheep in the wild in western North Dakota primarily along the Little Missouri River in the North Dakota Badlands.

Randy Kreil is Chief of Wildlife for North Dakota's Game and Fish Department.

Randy: Sheep have very good eyesight and they do put themselves in positions to see things.

Since 1950, when bighorns were introduced into the Badlands, North Dakota's Game and Fish Department has struggled with the job of managing an animal they knew little about.

Randy: Bighorn sheep are relatively long lived animals but their reproductive success is threatened. And it is limited not so much by the ewes getting pregnant and having the lambs, but it's the number of lambs that survive long enough to escape predators like coyotes and golden eagles.

Any answers about bighorns always leads to more questions? How many sheep are really out there? Where do they live? What do they eat? The biggest question is: who would pay the price for helping the bighorns survive? The answer? Hunters.

It's a fund raising night in Minneapolis for the Foundation for North American Wild Sheep, the Minnesota/Wisconsin chapter. The room is full of sheep hunters with sheep fever. Every item sold is money for wild sheep. But the most exciting bid of the night is still to come. One license to hunt a North Dakota bighorn.

Randy: It was back in about the mid 1980s that we started a partnership with the national organization of the Foundation for North American Wild Sheep. The hunting license was auctioned off at their national banquet. The price has ranged from $20,000 to $50,000 for the chance to hunt sheep.

All of the license money goes to manage North Dakota's wild sheep program. And look who's here? Pete Cimellaro. Bidding on behalf of his friend, Jimmy.

Auctioneer: Sold.

Jimmy: I bid $20,000 and I got it for $20,000. I thought this was a steal (laughs).

No stiff leg, no frozen knee, no hill or gully can discourage Jimmy Jamison from his $20,000 hunt for a North Dakota bighorn sheep.

Pete: I wish people could experience the passion that we have for these animals and the very few animals that we hunt are indeed surplus animals. We care about these sheep deeply. We recognize that if we're not involved in these programs, if we don't support them with our money, then they won't happen.

One more climb in the Badlands and Jimmy's luck quickly turned from poor to good. Moments later, one big ram veers off. And then, Jimmy's dream hunt came true.

Pete: He's an excellent bighorn. He's by far the largest taken this year.

Jimmy: It looked like it was going to be an easy hunt but it wasn't and they never are when you're hunting sheep.

Pete: I'm so thankful for the foundation and for guys like Jimmy who have the courage and the commitment to wild sheep.

If only the bighorns knew. If only Teddy Roosevelt knew. Things have gone from bad to good in the Badlands.

One more climb in the Badlands and Jimmy's
luck quickly turned from **poor to good**.
Moments later, one big ram veers off. And then,
Jimmy's **dream hunt** came true.

Meet Will Steger

If you're gonna make history about loving cold, surviving cold, being cold and living to tell about it, I guess it might as well be a Minnesotan. If so, Will Steger is a purebred. The sled dog exploration, led by Steger, to reach the North Pole was a true moment in history. Today, Will is a famed explorer but as heroes go he's shy about it. A true Minnesotan? Yah, you betcha.

Ron's Narrative: At first glance, there's nothing in Will Steger's boyhood pictures to suggest he was destined for the world's history book. Yet, there were hints. His mother remembers that young Will could simply never stay home.

Will Steger: I went down the Mississippi in my motor boat when I was 15 and I started climbing when I was 17 – I was allowed to fulfill those dreams.

Will's Mother: In high school, he would go on overnight trips and stuff like that, all over the country, we'd always let him go because it was a safer time.

Will: As a 4th grader, hockey was a big sport in Richfield and I traded my hockey skates for a sled load of national geographic magazines to read. That was what I wanted to do.

Ron Schara: Has Will Steger ever held a job, I mean have you ever punched a time clock?

Will: I did actually. I drove cabs, worked in factories and I also taught school for three years. But then I moved north and that was part of a calculated plan, I always knew I was going to move to the wilderness as a young kid.

So it comes as no surprise that Will Steger, explorer and lover of wilderness, has found another chunk of remote earth and another reason for pushing his spirit over more miles of God-awful ice, cold and snow.

Will: We're gonna cross the Barrens in the winter, I don't think that's ever been crossed in the winter. And then up north to Baffin Island where we'll cross the spine of Baffin down the ice caps and then eventually end up on the Atlantic Coast.

Adventure is Steger's middle name. In 1986, he led the world's first dogsled team ever to reach the North Pole. He also crossed Greenland in 1988 – the longest dogsled expedition in history. In 1989, he was the first to take a dogsled team across Antarctica. And now he's about to take the Arctic Transect.

Ron: Will this be the last hike?

Will: Well, I made the mistake of saying years ago this would be my last, I don't think I'll say that again.

Ron: You've made the history books, why risk life and limb? And why climb another mountain?

Will: This is a little different than climbing mountains and reaching the pole. Our civilization is facing some very serious environmental problems and as more science comes in we can see how our climate is really beginning to change.

And so…Will Steger went northbound once again…this time as Steger the teacher. Long ago he taught us about chasing dreams and testing the human spirit. Now he's testing our will to be stewards of mother earth.

Post Script: Like a fine clock, Will completed the Arctic Transect intact, including all who followed him. It was cold. It wasn't easy. And for Will Steger it was just perfect. In recent years, Will has led a one person campaign speaking to anyone, anywhere about the threat of global warning. Will is hoping we'll care enough to change the way we live. Why? His beloved north is melting away.

Adventure is Steger's middle name.

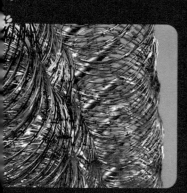

Prison Wild Flowers
PRAIRIE CORRECTIONAL FACILITY IN APPLETON, MINNESOTA.

Most of us can oohh and aaahh over
pretty flowers, especially native flowers
— black-eyed susans and the like. And we can
appreciate a horizon of tall prairie grasses,
waving in the wind. While our enthusiasm for
native prairie has grown, most of us rarely stop to think how
some of the restored prairie came to be.
That's why this story was so intriguing. Who would guess where
some of Minnesota's native prairie flowers first blossomed?

Ron's Narrative: On Big Stone National Wildlife Refuge in western Minnesota, prairie wild flowers once more bend in the wind. But restoring prairie isn't cheap. And refuge biologist, Ken Bosquet knows there's a price to be paid.

Ken Bosquet: To plant this field, the wildflower seedlings that we do can cost up to $200 or more per pound of wildflower seed. So, it is very expensive to just go out and purchase the seed. A field this size would cost about $6,000 or so in wildflower seed alone.

While the prairie winds are free. The wild flowers blowing in the breeze are now free in a different way. These flowers once grew in a Minnesota prison.

Female Guard: Cooper to master control – charley 6 alpha for 4 inmates 2 staff.

It is jail yard time at Prairie Correctional Facility in Appleton, Minnesota. But for these four inmates, Rodney, Anthony, Doug and Al, yard time is garden time. A wild flower garden.

Rodney: And this is a native prairie grass. This is what we want...that little head right there. A lot of seed in one of them little buds.

Prison Official Harvey Anderson oversees the prison prairie.

Harvey Anderson: This is a prairie cone flower. There's a lot of things happening inside this wire that the people on the outside don't realize. They don't just sit in their cells 24 hours a day doing nothing. And it's amazing how many people on the outside think that that's how a prison is run.

When they say, "I'm working with wild flowers," there's a sense of pride there and this is a result of what you see – of that pride.

Rodney: This the second year on these seeds too.

Harvey. Yeah.

Ron's Narrative: Meet Rodney. Prison time, 14 years. Growing wildflowers, two months.

Rodney: It helps, ease the mind and at least see the sun and the sky. A lot of people that are in max prisons only get outside, maybe an hour a day. And this gives me a chance to get outside at least four or five hours a day. So, it helps.

Meet Anthony. Prison time, 81 months.

Anthony: A lot of people here are good people who made a mistake. They can change and go on to do a lot of good things in this world.

Meet Al. Prison time, 8 years, 3 suspended.

Al: It's nice to know that you're giving something back. Basically, when I was on the outside, I had never seen any of this stuff out there.

Meet Doug. Sentenced to 10 years.

Doug: Even though I won't be able to drive down the road for a few more years, at least I'll know these flowers are out there somewhere.

Having prisoners grow and tend native wildflowers is an idea that sprouted in 2001 as a way to restore native prairie at Big Stone National Wildlife Refuge.

Refuge Official: Whatever seed that we can get from the prison is very beneficial for us. In the past we have been restoring about 250 acres per year and since the refuge was established in 1975 we have restored about 4,300 acres.

We are standing in a field that was planted with help from the prison gardeners. The main flowers are a grey-headed cone flower. There are some purple colors in here and the one in front is called Wild Burgemont or Bee Balm.

There was a time when western Minnesota had millions of acres of tall grass prairie. Now less than one percent of that original prairie remains.

But nobody can deny Minnesota is making progress. Today there's a small patch of prairie wildflowers growing where none grew before. And they are tended by hands that someday hope to be as free as the prairie wind.

A lot of people here are **good people who made a mistake.**
They can change and go on to do a lot of **good things** in this world.

Save the Turtle
WEAVER DUNES NATURE PRESERVE, WABASHA COUNTY, MINNESOTA

When it comes to **saving critters**, most of us get excited about wolves or loons and such. But who really can get excited about, say, a turtle? One day we answered our own question. We found folks **passionate** about being **turtle helpers**. Does it get any better?

Ron's Narrative: Every summer on Highway 84 in Wabasha County, Minnesota, while most of the traffic flies by, some of it races along at a turtle's pace. If you know your turtles – this is a Blanding's turtle. And it's crossing the road for a very good reason.

Jamie Edwards, DNR Turtle Helper: To get to the nesting islands on the other side.

Driven by the urge to lay its eggs, these Blanding's turtles leave the safety of a marsh to make a nest of eggs in sand. Sand on the other side of Highway 84. You see the Blanding's turtle in these parts is a pretty special turtle.

Turtle Helper: The neighbors have a lot of respect for them and they've taken some pride, in this turtle population. I think it's amazing – an amazing thing, to see this happen, to watch these turtles go across knowing exactly what they're going to do, lay their eggs. And they know to go across the road and to march back.

It so happens the sand the mama turtles are seeking is part of the Weaver Dunes Nature Preserve. In fact, the Dunes may attract the largest concentration of Blanding's in the country.

Turtle Helper: The Blanding's turtle has a distinctive yellow neck. And a dome shaped shell, it kind of looks like an army helmet. The population is estimated to be about 5,000 Blanding's turtles and that is just Blanding's, if you count all the turtle species, there may be 20,000 turtles in this area.

Trekking to the nesting grounds isn't especially easy if you're a turtle. And once there, most of the turtle's eggs – 80 to 90 percent – are eaten by predators before they hatch.

Turtle Helper: Digging in the sand – here's the nest cavity. It has been dug up and the shell fragments have been ripped up.

Worse yet, mama turtle has to cross the road again to return home. If only folks would brake for turtles.

Turtle Helper: You would hope the turtles would hurry up when they see a car coming. But that's not what they do. They just kind of stop and wonder what's happening.

But cars do slow down here. They know the turtles need a brake.

Turtle Helper: People in this community seem to know. The DNR has posted a sign to slow down. It's just like in the city – the pedestrians get the right of way. Here it's the turtle.

So, next time you're driving down Highway 84, remember to slow down. A turtle is somebody's mother.

The Blanding's turtle in these parts is a pretty special turtle.

Saving the Minnesota River

MINNESOTA RIVER

Spend a few minutes with Scott Sparlin and you know he's not joking. The Minnesota River needs help and he's the guy who can bring it. Yet, I was skeptical. Here was a guy who played dance music in bars by night and then fought to save a river by day? Who could do such a thing? We decided to find out by spending a day with Scott Sparlin, the River Man.

Ron's Narrative: It's the river that bears a special name – Minnesota. The Minnesota River. It's a river that on this morning appears postcard pretty, a river teeming with fish for the catching. And a river worth singing about.

Meet the river's pied piper – his name? Scott Sparlin. Have guitar, will sing. He's been singing for 30 years. Songs and words to make us clean up his favorite river.

Scott Sparlin: Water defines Minnesota, it keeps us going. It's a huge part of what we are – yet, the Minnesota River is the forgotten river.

The Minnesota River actually begins in western Minnesota, at Big Stone Lake. From there it begins a journey of 335 miles flowing south as well as north and ending in the Mississippi River at Fort Snelling in the Twin Cities.

But the Minnesota is also a troubled river. Troubled with pollution and litter.

To Scott Sparlin, litter is something he and others can do something about. On a Saturday in New Ulm, folks gather for an event they call Community Cleanup for Water Quality.

Nothing's glamorous about a river cleanup. Nothing's fun either. But these folks all believe they can make a difference.

Scott: That's 100 bags! We're cleaning up the river, one bag at a time. We're being proactive, rather than reactive and getting the phosphorus out before it gets into the water ways.

Rain water run off from farm fields also is a major source of chemical pollutants. A federal program called CREP – Conservation Reserve Enhancement Program – is paying landowners to protect the river and its watersheds.

Farmer: If you're 50 years old and planting oak trees, you know it's not for yourself. It's for your grandkids and nephews and for all of Minnesota.

Scott is also pushing other communities along the river's route to seek change.

Scott: The once forgotten river is being rediscovered.

And guess what? Fishing on the Minnesota River is coming back, too.

Angler: There are so many species in the river, but catfish are number one. Right now there are more fish in the river than I've seen in 30 years.

There was a time, when a Minnesota River catfish wasn't made for a frying pan. Now Scott doesn't mind eating a fish or two.

Scott: Mmmmm, that's a piece of heaven, a Minnesota River catfish at its best.

Yes, history has not been kind to the Minnesota River, but today there's new hope flowing from town to town, bank to bank. And someday, perhaps, the Minnesota River will look as it did in 1833 when described by an early explorer "As we paddled along, clouds of ducks and wild rice, our guide told us about the herds of bison that once roamed the river edge."

Today only bones of the bison remain.

Scott: I hope to see more of us using the river. I want to live to see more fishing and less pollution.

And maybe bison grazing again where the river flows.

Shirley's Land
CUSHING, MINNESOTA

Sometimes the star of our television stories are folks we've never met. For example, we never met Shirley Robinson. But her story is alive and well. And we wanted to tell it. If you enjoy nature and the outdoors, the greatest contribution anybody can make is to set aside some wild space for wild creatures. Shirley died way too young, but in death, that's what she did. She left a memory for her loved ones and for us that represents what she loved.

So, this was both a sad story, yet a happy one, too. I'm sure Shirley understands.

Mike Robinson: Shirley and I planted all the rice and then up north here there's another pond right over here, Shirley and I built that and then over there by that pine we built that one.

Ron's Narrative: To a visitor, this wild looking piece of land near Cushing, Minnesota is just a chunk of woods, brush and critters. But not anymore.

Now this land is dedicated to something else: a living memory of Shirley J. Robinson.

Mike: Shirley and I both worked at this place very hard. I have roots here and Shirley was a school teacher in Little Falls, Minnesota when we met. She was very much an outdoor gal and we both participated in everything whether it was a food plot for the deer – I'd drive the tractor and she'd go sew the seed or if we were building a damn, she was right there with the shovel next to me. Anything that has been done here Shirley did half the work.

Shirley loved this place until – just two miles down the road, she was killed in a tragic car accident.

A Friend: Shirley was just a wonderful person, she loved her students, she loved her husband Mike and she loved the environment.

After Shirley's death, her husband Mike made a tough decision. He sold the land – cheap – to be preserved by the Nature Conservancy and the Minnesota Department of Natural Resources.

DNR Official: It's tremendously important to Mike. Not only did he make a very significant financial contribution to making this happen – I mean if he hadn't done what he did we probably wouldn't be here today, because nobody could have afforded to pay what a realtor might have paid him for this land.

Now this land is the Shirley Robinson Memorial Refuge – including Shirley's final resting place.

A Friend: Now Mike has a very precious way of remembering his wife where her memory will not only be something of his, but something everyone else can appreciate as well.

Mike: I had to honor her. I could not let it be just developed – that would be just the opposite of what she wanted and also the opposite of what I wanted. She was loving and caring to her children and to her friends. I was lucky to have met her.

For Shirley... Her land is now forever wild.

Shirley was just a wonderful person.

A Cardinal Fan

Who cannot find joy in the sight of a cardinal? Not I. Cardinals have been my favorite bird for as long as I can remember. I was a St. Louis Cardinal fan, not because of Stan Musial, but because of the uniform insignia he wore...the cardinals sitting on a bat. In truth, I didn't really know that much about cardinals, the bird, as they almost always show up at bird feeders at the last light of day. All the more reason to do this story. Now we all can be cardinal fans.

In the stark environs of a Minnesota winter, we can all agree.
It's welcomed sight in any tree.
A day brightener dressed in crimson feathers.
A touch of the tropics on the tundra.

Famed Minnesota flyer, Charles Lindbergh, once said if he could choose he'd rather have birds than airplanes.

Behold the cardinal.
A favorite among we who cannot fly.
An icon of seven states and countless sport teams.
A bird so richly red, adorned with a noble crest, it was named in honor of Roman Catholic Cardinals who wore much the same.

Although the female cardinal is less showy and more drab, nature's way of camouflaging a red bird, together the cardinal pair who mate for life are true residents, winter or summer. Spring or fall.
And they frequent our backyards, attracted to bird feeders offering black sunflower seeds, cracked corn and other goodies.

Cardinals are notorious early and late in the day visitors to backyard handouts. Their short, stout beaks are designed for breaking seeds or crushing bugs.

Aesop, the philosopher once said, "It is not only fine feathers that make fine birds."

The good news is fine birds seem to be expanding their range in America, spreading both north and west in brushy habitats.

So — God speed to the red bird of happiness.

To paraphrase poet, Emily Dickinson, "If you love cardinals, it saves going to heaven."

It's a **welcome sight** in any tree.

A Magic River

OTTER TAIL RIVER, MINNESOTA

We tend to ignore our rivers because we have too many lakes. That's good if you're in the television business. It means there are many rivers to explore because viewers have never explored them before. Such is the case of the Otter Tail River. A DNR fishery fella, Henry Drewes, first tipped me off about the Otter Tail. He said it was a great smallmouth river that nobody knew, except a few. If you are reading, now it's not so few.

Ron's Narrative: A half century ago, Laura Gilpin, an American author whose name has drifted downstream in the current of time, was enamored by rivers. "A river seems a magic thing," she wrote.

River Fisherman: Here he comes. Whoa, he's a big dude.

Today the magic still flows.

River Fisherman: Welcome to the Otter Tail.

The Otter Tail. A Minnesota river whose name covers 195 river miles of countless lakes and a colorful county with the same name. As we launch our fishing canoes below an old power dam, the Otter Tail quickly shows its many faces. My fishing partner, Bill Plantan, loves them all.

Bill Plantan: Look at 'em, – he's a dandy – my hand is 9 inches and that's about 17.

If you're an adventuring angler, it's easy to love rivers that harbor smallmouth bass – a fish built like a football and just as tough.

Bill: Whoa, holy cow, that sounded big – he's huge!

After fighting the river's brush as well as the bass, the ending was a happy one.

Bill: He's 20 inches on the nose.

Quickly the river's joy spread as my brother, Rick Schara, tangled with yet another football.

Bro' Rick Schara: Oh my golly, look at the size of that one. How many inches – he's at least 18. That's the Otter Tail.

The Otter Tail's smallie smorgasbord, we discovered wasn't by accident.

Arlin Schalekamp, DNR Fish Biologist: We did habitat improvement projects. We've done bank stabilization projects, it's got water quality, it's got a good forage base, and the catch and release regulations really helped.

Back in 1992, DNR fish managers stocked a mere 230 adult smallmouth in the Otter Tail River upstream from Fergus Falls.

Arlin: It didn't take much, they're pretty aggressive colonizers and there were no predators in the stream – the habitat was here and they just took off.

The smallmouth also found themselves in a river with stretches seemingly untampered by man.

Arlin: Right here it's kind of free and wild, it kind of resembles what the river looked like 100 or 200 years ago. As you move down stream it becomes more of a prairie stream.

On this day, no matter where the river led us, swift or slow, the smallmouth were already there.

Bill: That's a beauty Ron – quick release, nice job.

If we had any doubts about the success of the DNR's fish restoration projects, the Otter Tail's smallmouth swept them away.

Bill: Just another Otter Tail smallmouth – just a beauty.

Just like magic.

All About Blue Jays

It must be human nature but there are some wild critters we'd rather dislike than adore. I can think of wood ticks, as an example. Among the birds we know, lots of folks **can't stand Blue Jays.** Maybe it's their **brash manners and loud mouth.** Yet, I suspect, there's something loveable about Blue Jays if only we knew.

One day one of our videographers, Nick Clausen, said he'd spotted a Blue Jay nest in his backyard. So Nick rigged a small camera next to the nest and periodically recorded the life and times of Blue Jay parents **struggling to raise a family.** Suddenly, we had a different view toward Blue Jays. They are only trying to do what every wild creature tries to do...and that is to survive.

We needed to change our attitudes toward Blue Jays.

After all, our story showed Blue Jays have mothers, too.

Ron's Narrative: If there's such a bird as a loud mouth. Or a bird with bad table manners. Or a birdy bad reputation. This bird of a feather has 'em all.

Ron Schara: There's your Blue Jay...look straight up, you'll see him sitting on the branch...he's getting nervous already. He wants those peanuts – from that peanut feeder.

Naturalist and wildlife photographer Stan Tekiela has clicked his shutter on lots of birds. Most of them, aaah, well-behaved and nice birds.

Stan Tekiela: The yellow one is an American Gold Finch, and the red ones are house finches. Oh, there's a hairy woodpecker.

Blue Jays on the other hand tend to be troublemakers.

Stan: A lot of people don't like Blue Jays because they think they're out taking other bird eggs or babies. I'm not sure why Blue Jays are singled out. In nature that's how it is...it is survival and that's what they do.

A Blue Jay is also somebody's mother.

Stan: Both parents take turns sitting on the eggs and sitting on the babies. And this is an activity that most people aren't aware of – that the parents will sit on the young and keep them warm. They'll stay in the nest about 2 weeks to 17 days feeding. They feed them a diet of insects, so they have a lot of protein and they grow very quickly.

As Willie might say, don't let your cardinals grow up to be Blue Jays.

But nature is nature, not a song, not a court.

So let us not judge the bird by some avian tort.

Sometimes we're mistaken; and I'll give you a clue.

A Blue Jay has feathers but they're not really blue.

Blue Jays may be loudmouths, trouble on a twig.

But they're smart and they're pretty. Traits we can dig.

Just remember, a Blue Jay has a maker. One that we share.

What if we had to sit in treetops

While the Blue Jay enjoyed a chair?

All About Hummingbirds

If you do stories about swans, how can you pass up a story about hummingbirds? Especially at a place where hummingbirds gathered by the dozens. To see such a dainty bird and to marvel about how it survives — these are some of the ingredients for our eternal search for nature's questions and her answers.

Ron's Narrative: It's the world's smallest air show. And it arrives in John Weissenburger's backyard as the days of summer wind down. They are hummingbirds. Specifically, Ruby throated hummingbirds. And they are so tiny.

A mere three and one half inches long, and weighing less than 2-tenths of an ounce, it's the only hummingbird that lives in Minnesota.

John Weissenburger: I've been feeding them since 1988.

John's handout is pure sugar water. He goes through about eight pounds of sugar in six weeks.

John: It seems like you start out with very few. Then, they must communicate with each other because pretty soon, it's kinda like the baseball movie saying if you build it they will come. Well, if you feed them they will come.

On this day they came by the dozens. Starting around August 1st Weissenburger's backyard turns into a busy airport filled with dozens of olive colored females along with male birds identified by their bright ruby throats.

Hummingbirds are perfectly named. Their wings hum at an incredible speed of 80 times a minute. But that's slow compared to the bird's heart rate of 1260 beats a minute. A human heart beats only 70 to 80 times a minute.

The bird's ability to start, stop and fly instantly at 50 miles per hour in any direction is an aviation wonder.

John: It's kinda like a happy hour around here sometimes. At times I've had 16 birds actually perched on the feeders and another 16 buzzing around trying to land.

Despite their miniature size, hummingbirds are not docile flyers.

John: They make a lot of racket and they'll chase each other. They're just really fascinating to watch.

When the days turn from August to September, the flying show eventually disappears. The tiny birds know enough to head south to Central America to spend the winter, although it's a 500-mile flight across the Gulf of Mexico. To a hummingbird, no sweat. Just a few million wing flaps.

If you feed them, they will come.

All About Wood Ticks

Simply say the word, wood tick. And your hair starts crawling. At least my hair does. Now I've been **a victim a time or two** so I have every reason not to like wood ticks. But maybe there was something I didn't know about wood ticks. Do they have mothers? **Family reunions?** So, we decided to find out, going forth with crawling skin, to tell the story of wood ticks.

Ron's Narrative: In nature, they say, there are no villains. Hmmm. So, how do we explain wood ticks?

Jeff Hahn, Wood Tick Expert: A wood tick is also known as the American dark tick. It's not an insect as some people might think; it's related to spiders.

Ron Schara: Okay, let's get to the point – Is there possibly anything nice to say about wood ticks?

Jeff: Wood ticks are not harmful – they are an annoyance because they bite.

Ron: Are we supposed to like having our blood sucked away?

Jeff: This is a critter that needs blood to survive

So the female needs blood to lay eggs. Why bother me? I've tried, but frankly, I can't think of one compliment to give to a wood tick. And now there's another tick, the deer tick, that spreads lyme disease. Is that nice? In Minnesota, lyme disease cases have jumped by 88 percent in one year. Just the sight of a tick gives me goose bumps. How are you supposed to respect something that gives you goose bumps? Even wood ticks who are minding their own business give me the creeps.

Some people have really bad tick fears. Just say wood tick and their hair begins to itch from their head to their crotch. When you think a tick might be heading north of your knees, the feeling really gets bad. You want to go crazy. You itch all over. It's an awful thing. I've had ticks hanging on me in places I can't even see.

Worse, tick bites are almost painless. You don't feel a thing when a tick drills for your blood. And once its head is buried in your hide, removing said tick is far from easy. Pull gently the experts say. Of course, it never works that easy.

A poet, O.G. Harmon, told it like it is:

If you get sufficient hold,
To fetch it with a sudden start.
It not infrequently occurs,
The wood tick's head and body part.

Beheading wood ticks sounds terrible, but frankly the ticks deserve it.

Have you ever seen animal rights folks march for the ethical treatment of wood ticks?

Just the sight of a tick gives me goose bumps.

Dance of the Western Grebes

LAKE OSAKIS, MINNESOTA

Nature does work in strange ways. And one of the strangest takes place in the spring on a prairie lake we call Osakis. For reasons unknown, Osakis is a gathering place for the Western Grebe, a bird with one of the most animated courtship dances in the bird world. What's more, Osakis may be the only lake in Minnesota where it takes place in such a grand ballroom style. We arrived early to watch it happen.

Ron's Narrative: Sunrise on Lake Osakis. This is not just another Minnesota fishing lake. On this dawn Osakis is more like a symphony hall. A symphony conducted by mother nature with an orchestra of grebes and gulls and so many other nameless sounds.

It's a magical melody that echoes over Lake Osakis on this morning. And a rare one. This is the Western Grebe. As its name implies, it is a bird commonly found in western states but it is apparently spreading eastward.

Don Enger, Wildlife Photographer: When we first came to Lake Osakis in 1959, we didn't have any Western Grebes. I would say they started to come here in the early 80's. There weren't nearly as many then as we have now.

Amazingly, Lake Osakis is now home to one of the largest concentrations of Western Grebes east of the Rocky Mountains. Why the grebes have chosen Osakis, nobody knows for sure, except Osakis is rich in fish life and grebes are avid fish eaters.

Some lake residents worry the grebes are eating too many fish.

Naturalist: I think for a lot of people it's sort of a catch 22 situation. I've watched these grebes for many years and I honestly think it's not detrimental as far as the fishing is concerned.

Indeed, Osakis may be the most birdy lake in Minnesota. Forester terns fill the air. Pelicans skim the surface. The brightly-dressed yellow headed blackbird flits amid the cattails.

Yet, the most impressive feathered resident, the Western Grebe, has a long white neck, a black cap and a red eye. And its courtship song echoes over Osakis every spring.

Naturalist: As soon as the ice goes out on Lake Osakis, watch for the grebes. But don't expect to see them in the air.

As you can see they're pretty much shaped like a bullet and they're fantastic flyers. But during the mating season they don't fly at all.

Instead, the Western Grebe prefers to dance. And dance. And dance.

Naturalist: It starts with lots of bobbing heads and busy necks.

As the grebe symphony plays, the dance soon begins.

First one dance and then another. Some say the dance resembles outboard chickens. It's all for courtship, of course.

Naturalist: When they find their mate and begin to build a nest, that's when they go down and pick up weeds and come together and do the weed dance.

When its time to nest, grebes don't mind company with nests of two to four eggs side by side on floating mats of vegetation. When hatched, young grebes catch a ride on their mother's back and until they learn to swim, that's where they stay.

Naturalist: One day in October you'll wake up one morning and there will not be a single grebe on the lake. They leave at night.

And the symphony of grebes goes silent, not to be heard again on Osakis, until spring returns

As the grebe **symphony** plays,
the **dance** soon begins.

How Birds Fly

How birds fly in nature, we tend to take things for granted. Things like flying. For this reason, we decided to do a story as basic as how birds fly. Birds have many marvelous adaptations that allow them to soar with impunity. I also knew the University of Minnesota had a Natural History Museum full of bird skeletons, bird skins and bird feathers. By combining the bird stuff with selections of great bird video taken by our staff, we had a great story. And now everybody knows...how birds fly.

Ron's Narrative: Airplanes fly. Mighty fast, if it's an F-16.

Many insects have wings, too.

But through the wild blue yonder, nothing flies like birds fly.

Birds are the original flying machines.

U of M Bird Expert: The magic of flight comes to me when I see a jet fighter fly by, and I think they look a lot like a bird, then I realize hey wait a minute, they look a lot like a bird, because birds are models of aerodynamic efficiencies and we actually copied them.

Everything about a bird seems designed to take off.

Here at the University of Minnesota's Ecology Hall, a bird's skeleton reveals the secrets of flight. The bones of birds, for example, are designed to be strong yet light.

U of M Bird Expert: If you want to make an efficient flying machine, you don't have a large amount of weight on the wings or head or tail, you have to centralize it in the core.

No modern birds have teeth, and you have to find a way to grind up your food if you don't have teeth. The modern bird solution is to have a gizzard – it is a muscle organ centralized in the body that grinds up food.

And being light as a feather is no accident.

U of M Bird Expert: When we look at feathers we see they are lightweight, they are strong and water repellent and they make good propellers, we see the way they are arranged in the wing, in such a way, that the outer part of the wing consists of the primary feathers and the inner part is the secondary, and the bottom provides the "get" and top the "go."

Mankind has marveled at flight for centuries, of course. Perhaps that more than anything explains our continuing fascination with birds.

At the University some 50,000 bird skins and 6,000 bird skeletons line these drawers and boxes.

They are like the only copy of a rare book in a library.

Our search for bird secrets hasn't really changed much, however.

Birds still fly.

While the rest of us wonder – why, oh why, can't I?

But through the wild blue yonder, nothing flies like birds fly.

Meet the Gray Jay

If there's such a thing as reincarnation, I'd like to come back as a Gray Jay. These birds have life figured out. Most creatures run from us. One whiff of us and a deer bolts. One word and a duck flushes. If it's wild, it runs away. But not the Gray Jay. You have to go to northern Minnesota and beyond to meet a Gray Jay. But it's worth it. Sit down at a table outside in the pines.

But do keep an eye on your sandwich.

Ron's Narrative: Sometimes when you go north, you'll know it without a compass, without a snowy ride through the conifers. Nature will tell you when you're really north.

You're up north when the Gray Jay appears. It is a bird with lots of different names. Whiskey Jack. Camp Robber. Moose Bird. So many names because the bird has been company to so many travelers. It's almost magical. Just pause in the woods and a Gray Jay will show up at your side as if it knew you were coming. A welcome wagon greeter in feathers.

But there's a reason for all of this birdie hospitality.

The bird's boldness is part of another agenda.

In a word, survival.

The Ojibwa called it Wiskedjak. And according to Indian lore, the bird is very sly, almost a human in gray feathers.

The north might be pretty to look at, but in winter it's a harsh world. And even the big critters, like a wandering moose, will not find life easy. Imagine what it's like when you're hungry and all you've got are sharp eyes and an even sharper beak.

The Gray Jay thinks nothing of helping itself to anybody's food. Thus the name, Camp Robber.

But survival is not a crime in the north. In early spring, the Gray Jay begins nesting, despite lingering snow banks and cold temperatures. That is when the bird will remember all of the tidbits it has tucked away amid the treetops.

It's no wonder Gray Jays seem to relish your company. You're the answer to survival.

Just **pause in the woods** and a Gray Jay
will show up **at your side**
as if it knew you were coming.

Minnesota's Symbols

We all know Minnesota has a wide variety of plants and wildlife. Some time ago, the Minnesota legislature decided that some of these plants and animals meant more to us than others. Thus began an official state list of such creatures.

We begin with the loon. It was Minnesota's first state animal symbol, a bird that means water and lakes. The loon also makes Minnesota's most famous call of the wild. More loons live and nest in our Minnesota lakes than in any other state, except Alaska. Loons also fit in with our lifestyle. They are excellent swimmers and feed on fish, sometimes diving to extreme depths. Built like a boat, loons appear awkward walking on land.

But it's the call of the loon that moves us, a call that conjures up images of wilderness at its best. That's probably the main reason the legislature voted in 1961 to designate the loon as our state bird.

The Minnesota state fish is golden in color and golden delicious in a frying pan. No other state raises more walleyes than Minnesota. Famed for its catching fun and eating fun, the walleye actually is a member of the perch family. The name, walleye, comes from the appearance of its glassy eye, which by the way makes for excellent night vision. Minnesotans consume about 4 million pounds of walleye every year. All the more reason the fish became an official Minnesotan back in 1965.

When you think of the north woods of the Minnesota, the pine tree comes to mind. That may explain why the state tree is the Red Pine also known as the Norway Pine. They grow mainly in the northern part of the state. There's a great collection of Red Pine at Minnesota's first state park, Itasca, including the state's tallest at 126 feet and it is estimated to be more than 200 years old. The Red Pine was selected as our state tree in 1953.

Minnesota was the first state to have an official fungi. Yes, fungi. It's the famed **morel mushroom**, our official fungi since 1984. Many folks consider morels an elusive but wonderful woodland treat. The prime time for morel hunting starts in early May. They range from 2 to 6 inches tall, appearing like a sponge on a stalk. Good places to find 'em are below dying elm and in old apple orchids. Remember, never eat a wild mushroom that you're not sure of — take the advice of an expert — when in doubt throw it out.

Our state flower has three names...the showy **Lady Slipper** also known as the pink and White Lady Slipper. It's one of 45 orchids native to Minnesota, and it sorta does look like a woman's slipper. They bloom

best in sunny damp areas such as a swamps and bogs. It must live 14 to 20 years before it blooms for the first time. But don't even think about picking our state flower. It's illegal. Besides, the Lady Slipper left alone will grow to be 100 years old or more.

Rock hounds know the state gemstone is the **agate.** If you look hard enough for agates, you're apt to get a case of aga-tites. The Lake Superior agate is one of the oldest rocks known to mankind. The Superior agate is often found on gravel beaches along Lake Superior. Named the official gemstone in 1969, agates are an historic symbol of Minnesota, ranging from ancient volcanoes to aged glaciers to the iron ore that once provided so many jobs in northern Minnesota.

Together, the various state symbols mean one more thing. In Minnesota, if you look long enough, **you'll find the good life.**

Mr. and Mrs. Robin

Sometimes the best stories are right under your nose. Or, in my case, under the house deck. There they were, Mr. and Mrs. Robin doing what robins do in springtime — building a nest and raising a family. This time we were ready with a miniature camera and recording deck.

Presto, we had a robin story that featured robins doing stuff nobody knew robins did.

This robin story also is another landmark of sorts. It's the only video in the history of Minnesota Bound that was shot by me. Well, that's not quite the truth. Let's just say, I pushed the record button when the robins were doing something interesting.

Ron's Narrative: America's bird is the American Robin. Its red breast is as familiar as the flag. Its lifestyle – an early bird gets the worm – is the American way. And, it's everybody's first sign of spring in America because the robin hops in every yard – in every state, excluding Hawaii.

Yes, we are robin enriched. The bird makes us sing. The red robin comes a bop, bop, bopping along.

Or inspires us to verse. Here is what one poet wrote:

There was a little robin
Whose head was always bobbin
Who said as he gobbled up a worm
I have swallowed all your brothers and 37 others
And goodness how they tickle
When they squirm.

Robins may be common but they are not ordinary.

Among those birds who migrate, scientists say, the robin is a slow flyer, going 30 to 40 miles per day. A robin heading to Alaska for the summer may take 80 days to fly 3,000 miles.

As parents, however, there's nothing slow about robins. Young are hatched in less than 14 days and the dutiful father and mother spend their days tending the young, usually three or more.

They show up with a beakful of worms and, presto, three gaping mouths await.

They feed one end first. Then clean up the other end. Oh, the joys of parenthood.

When a baby robin goes potty, it comes out in a white sack to keep the nest clean. It's the father and mother's job to fly it out or take it down.

And when it rains? Mama comes to the rescue, spreading her wings like an umbrella over her precious triplets.

In a matter of days, the fuzzy babies begin to grow feathers and orange breasts. Suddenly the nest isn't big enough for everybody. And the dangers of life begin to increase.

Don't fall – Oh that was close.

Three days later the dutiful parents were literally empty nesters. And they seemed shocked by the emptiness. Time perhaps to reshape the nest for the next family.

Poet Francis Duggan once observed:

The nest of a robin
And his faithful wife
A memory to carry
And to cherish for life.

The most vivid autumn scarlet to feast our eyes.

Ode to the Sumac

The autumn season is a menagerie of sights, sounds and smells. There are so many rushes to our senses, it's not surprising that we probably overlook some of the fall splendor. Or we simply take it for granted. It was thoughts like these that prompted us to examine one of autumn's most vivid players, the Sumac bush.

Ron's Narrative: In the autumn of our lives, we relish the music of wild geese…we soak in the splendor of Tamarack trees…we praise the grace of migrating swans.

But what about the lowly Sumac. No poetic tributes. No ode to the most vivid autumn scarlet to feast our eyes.

Oh lovely sumac, it's time we got to know you. Two kinds of Sumac – staghorn and smooth, always seem to grow in just the right spaces…turning our roadsides into pretty places.

There's a third kind of Sumac, one to beware. But poison Sumac is rare and grows in wet places where we seldom walk. Keep your boots dry and you'll get by.

Just remember – friendly Sumac has red berries; and good berries they are. Full of Vitamin C. Native Americans and pioneers turned the Sumac's crimson fruit into medicinal wine or a tasty drink, sweetened with honey from honey bees.

Historians say Sumac leaves and bark once helped us tan leather, dye our clothes and cure ailments ranging from diarrhea to gonorrhea. Maybe that's more about Sumac than we needed to know.

Maybe it's enough to know – that of all the greenery of summer, it's the Sumac that heralds a changing season. Its tropical leaves transform like magic into blades of fire. So ends the Sumac's cycle. Winter nears, its beauty fades and only Sumac seeds remain. Seeds to feed the birds. Seeds to start anew. Seeds to start another patch of autumn eye candy.

Oh Sumac, that's my ode to you.

Song of the Loon

Of all our feathered friends, this seems to be America's bird. Well-dressed in formal feathers. With haunting eyes that glow like a red sunrise. But what a name. Loon.

Loon as in what Scandinavians might call lum or lummox, meaning clumsy. Even Shakespeare referred to the loon as a fool because on land the loon walks like a drunk. But on the water, they are pure grace.

Rich Baker, Loon Expert: Having their feet way back like that, allows them to be great swimmers, it's like having a propeller in the back of the ship.

Ron's Narrative: A loon must be quick underwater when the main course is small fish. So flying becomes secondary.

Rich: You don't often see them getting airborne because they don't bother to fly very often.

To most of us, the loon is more than a bird, however. It's a legend. Indian tribes heard the loon as the voice of the earth's spirit-creator. It's also one of the earth's first bird species, scientists say. Evolving millions of years ago. Ironically, loons also have solid rather than hollow bones which are better suited for diving than flying.

But of all the loon lore, it's the voice that's most compelling. Its songs are mysterious and wild.

Naturalist: I think they evoke some sense of wildness.

Naturalist Aldo Leopold once said, the Lord did well when he put the loon and his music in the land. A loon typically has four different calls, the wail, the tremelo, the yodel and a loon hoot of contentment. Outside of Alaska, Minnesota is home to more loons than any other state.

In the meantime, the loons do their thing. Only loons know males from females – only loons can dive to 200 foot depths and come up without gasping.

And always they sing. Reminding us of wild places, of haunting solitude, of mystic memories.

Naturalist: Their call is kind of haunting, but it is just beautiful and it's very special.

A special song that touches us. A song perhaps from whence we came.

Indian tribes heard the loon as the
voice of the earth's spirit-creator.

The Amazing Dragonfly

If you've ever spent time next to water, wading a stream or sitting on a lake bank, it's likely you've been amazed by dragonflies. As a kid raised on trout fishing, I spent many hours in the company of these flying dragons. My most memorable encounter with a dragonfly happened one day while I was casting a dry fly into Minnesota's Hay Creek. While I'm not the best flycaster in hipboots, suddenly my forward cast became discombobulated as if I'd hooked an oak leaf. What was fluttering on the end of my line? The answer was...a dragonfly. It had attacked the artificial fly that was whipping around on the end of my flyline, thinking it might be an easy meal. From that day forth, I realized the speed and agility of dragonflies.

Later, I met scientists who shared my fascination and I met Chuck Carmichael, an entrepreneur who thought the sound of dragonflies might work to keep mosquitoes away.

Ron's Narrative: From the moment it takes off, nothing in the air flies like a dragonfly.

Up, down and around, forward and backward in the blink of its many eyes.

Dragonflies have been flying with the right stuff for more than 200 million years, scientists say. Four wings each controllable for aerial acrobatics.

Some 400 species of dragonflies rule the skies over North America and each takes off for one purpose: to catch and eat other flying insects.

Entomologist: They do eat a lot of mosquitoes...what's interesting about dragonflies is they will catch food in mid-flight and they'll eat for instance a mosquito while they are flying.

Yes, they eat in the air – they even mate in the air. They only return to earth to lay eggs.

Entomologist: They are harmless to humans and they do not bite – if they are diving towards you, it's because you maybe have mosquitoes around your body.

In fact, some folks refer to the dragonfly as a mosquito hawk.

Chuck Carmichael, Minnesota Entrepreneur: They contribute enormously to decreasing the population of mosquitoes – they eat around 300 mosquitoes a day which is quite a bit.

Chuck Carmichael is a Minnesota entrepreneur who thinks the whirr of dragonfly wings might be the perfect mosquito repellent. Why? Is it possible that over thousands of years mosquitoes have learned to fear the sound of a dragonfly's beating wings?

Chuck: I'm setting up a testing area. I have 6 speakers – mid range speakers that you can use on your patio deck or on a camping trip. It would create a bug free zone and it would reduce the number of mosquitoes in your area.

To record the insect's beating wings, Chuck developed a dragonfly sound studio, of sorts.

Chuck: The recording is done by way of holding the dragonfly in a clip like this. It's sensitive to the legs of the dragonfly so it doesn't harm the insect. Then, I hold the dragonfly close to a microphone to record the beating wing sound.

Will it work? Skeptics don't think so. But Chuck Carmichael is not dismayed.

Chuck: There are things out there that haven't been tested and haven't been tried to control mosquitoes and we gotta look for those. Instead of using chemicals, let's use something different – like audio – something that is comfortable with the environment instead of destroying it.

But questions remain. After thousands of years of flying together, will mosquitoes fear the sounds of dragonfly wings?

Entomologist: Mosquitoes probably wouldn't care if they heard dragonfly wings or not. Their main purpose is to find blood protein so they can lay their eggs. Even from what I've read about mosquitoes swarming, dragonflies will fly right through them and it doesn't faze the mosquitoes.

Chuck: We always have to try something. And you never know – maybe something will work. I'm just one of those people trying to change the way we think.

In the meantime, dragonflies do what they've always done. Scouring the skies to snare a meal of mosquitoes, deer flies and other biting pests. If you ask me, it's not United that makes for friendly skies, it's dragonflies.

From the moment it takes off,
nothing in the air flies like a dragonfly.

The Glorious Swan

Swans are pretty things. Everybody knows that. But until you've hung around swans, to watch them fly, to see them in the grand passage called migration, you really don't know how lucky we are to have swans in our lives. One day we learned that swans and the advances of civilization had found a common bond. On the Mississippi River, above the Twin Cities, a nuclear power plant was warming the water in late autumn and, inadvertently, creating a handy migratory pit stop for swans. Get the picture? We did.

Ron's Narrative: In all things of nature, Aristotle once noted, there is something of the marvelous. Perhaps Aristotle was looking at swans.

These are Trumpeter Swans, a wintering flock lollygagging in open water on the Mississippi River upstream from the Twin Cities.

Carrol Henderson, DNR Nongame Expert: Right now we are looking at a really wonderful success story with the restoration of Minnesota's Trumpeter Swans.

Gone from Minnesota's skies for more than a century, the DNR's non-game program began 24 years ago raising and releasing wild swans.

Carrol: Ten years ago we had less than 500 swans in the whole state. But now the population is up to more than 1,300 swans and is still growing by perhaps a couple hundred swans a year.

Eventually, these Trumpeter Swans will follow the Mississippi River as far south as Missouri and Arkansas to spend the winter. Until they do, Minnesota's Swan Lady keeps them company.

Sheila Lawrence, The Swan Lady: You want some?

These swans seem to know Sheila Lawrence and she them.

Sheila: There is a mute that is usually here and a couple tundras.

For 16 years, Sheila who lives along the river has taken the swans under her wing and offers free handouts of corn.

Sheila: The first year there were 15 that wintered here and each year it kept on increasing. Now I can't shut it off. But I like to watch them, they are so animated and big. They are an amazing bird to me.

Carrol: I think one of the most special stories about this is the citizens of Minnesota made this possible. On our state tax forms we have that little line with the loon on it and when people see that line – that's where they can make their annual donation to help Minnesota's wildlife.

Sheila: Swans are just so special. When you see them flap their wings, it reminds me of angel's wings.

They drift on still water, mysterious and beautiful, a poet once wrote.

By lake's edge or pool, they delight men's eyes. Then I awake someday to find they have flown away.

Centuries ago, we watched and wondered about swans, about something marvelous. Then, the swans almost disappeared. But now, we're lucky. We can marvel again.

When you see them flap their wings,
it reminds me of **angel's wings**

The Goofy Grouse

One of the most bazaar stories we've ever found in Minnesota turned out to be more than a one time story. It's about goofy grouse. These are wild grouse that come out of the woods and become attracted to our machines and to us. Nobody knows why a perfectly normal wild ruffed grouse will become enamored with lawn mowers or all-terrain vehicles, but they can.

We call this the case of the goofy grouse.

Ron's Narrative: In the north woods, ruffed grouse are supposed to fly away from us. And most of them do. But once upon a spring day in Tom Tesmar's backyard, the dangest thing happened.

Tom Tesmar: I was mowing the grass...and suddenly next to me was the bird.

For reasons known only to the bird, it had a thing for Tom's lawn tractor. In any direction, wherever the lawn tractor went, the bird was sure to follow. Never in nature, I swear, has there been such a sight.

And now the friendly bird has become a playmate for son, Thomas. He calls the bird Rufus.

Thomas: Come Rufus.

Thomas even talks to the bird and the bird talks back.

Thomas: What have you been doing? (bird chirps) I know you've been eating those green plants.

It seems Rufus first showed up when the lawn tractor started.

Tom: She's really amorous when the tractor starts.

Does it mean birds of a feather go put-put together.

But how do we explain the story of Rusty.

Roger Blavat: Rusty, come here Rusty.

You could say Rusty is an odd duck. Except Rusty is a ruffed grouse. One summer day Rusty walked out of the woods and, well, adopted the Roger Blavat family near Elk River, Minnesota. The bird was watching him, Roger said.

Roger: He just got closer and closer and before you knew it he just hopped right up on my leg. The grandkids just love him and he seems to like them, they'll play games with him and get him chasing them and roll the ball back and forth.

Rusty got so friendly he was a pain in the peck.

Roger: Every morning he's peaking through the window when you're having coffee. He'll peck on the window to get your attention. He wants you to come out.

And when we're leaving for work in the morning, he runs right out to the car and he'll literally chase the car down the driveway.

For unknown reasons, Rusty craved attention.

Roger: He's like a spoiled kid.

But this is a wild bird – a wild bird acting like a long lost companion who can only chirp.

Roger: I wish I knew what he was trying to say.

Nobody will ever know what Rusty or Rufus were trying to say. One day Rusty chased a car to close and was run over. And what about Rufus? Well, one day Rufus no longer answered the call of the lawn tractor.

Nobody knows why a perfectly normal wild ruffed grouse will become **enamored with lawn** mowers or all terrain vehicles but they can.

The Story of H99

In our constant hunt for stories to tell, sometimes we get lucky. One day we received a call from the U.S. Fish and Wildlife Service about a banded swan that had showed up in a zoo pond in Wisconsin. So begins this unusual swan story with an ending nobody expected.

Ron's Narrative: Of all the birds in our world, the Trumpeter Swan is a picture of feathered grace. Thirty pounds of poetry on 7-foot wings. In the air or on the water, it's been said, the bird appears like an armful of white blossoms.

Just like this one – a swan blossom known as H99 – so named by his neck collar. One day H99 landed here as an unexpected winter visitor at a zoo in Marshfield, Wisconsin.

Zoo Worker: It would have been about mid-December that we saw the Trumpeter come in and we knew it was kind of unusual.

Unusual turned out to be understatement. As we'll discover, H99 is a swan with a fairy tale.

Iowa Naturalist: This is where H99 was hatched. He was actually hatched out on this nesting platform – the female that you see out here without the collar is H99's mother.

H99's story begins in Iowa, here at a place known as the Grotto in West Bend. Hatched as a cygnet in 1999, H99 became part of Iowa's swan restoration program in the state's northwest corner.

A few years later, H99 blossomed into a beautiful male swan, who quickly found a free flying mate. Together, they flew north, across the border into Minnesota to a place called Sellner's Slough near Sleepy Eye, Minnesota. Come spring, it's time to make a nest and have a family.

Minnesota DNR Biologist: They raised 4 young. Sometimes the future of the population in an area may depend upon one really determined bird getting a mate and re-establishing in the area. Hopefully their young will return to the Prairie Pothole portion of Minnesota and establish their own nests. So, maybe the big picture starts with one bird – one really determined bird.

At the end of autumn, as Trumpeter Swans have done for centuries, H99 and his mate began a long journey south to their migratory home in Texas.

The saga of H99 had only begun.

Iowa Veterinarian: I got a call around Christmas of 2003 that a family of Iowa swans had been shot north of Lubbock, Texas.

Iowa Veterinarian: This is a picture of H99 when we got him. When he came up from Texas and he was already pretty stabilized by doctors. You can see he's got multiple shotgun pellets in him and he's got a pellet in this wing and over in that wing.

His mate killed by vandals, a severely injured H99 and one of his cygnets was returned to his roots, a wildlife rehabilitation center in Spirit Lake, Iowa. Center director, Linda Hinshaw remembers.

Linda Hinshaw: I think it's a miracle. Both birds had fractured wings and yet they were holding them symmetrically and flapping them symmetrically and the joints all looked good so we had really high hopes that both birds would at some future point in time be releasable.

And so it was, a recovered H99 soon flew away on his patched up 7-foot wings.

Wisconsin Zoo Keeper: Where ya going H?

To everyone's surprise, H99's next stop was here at the Marshfield, Wisconsin Zoo.

Zoo Keeper: I call him H for short. Around December 14th I heard that a Trumpeter had come in and had a fight with one of the mute swans that was on this pond. I think it's an odd place for a Trumpeter to winter but we feed them every day and he's pretty well taken care of here.

We sent the number in and started to get all this information back on the life history of this bird which is pretty extensive. My supervisor said we should call him lucky.

News of H99's whereabouts reached regional headquarters of the U.S. Fish and Wildlife Service (USFWS) back in Minnesota.

USFWS Biologist: I thought wow, this really makes my day. There's so much of what we do that is just processing paper work. It's an incredible journey that he's made and one can only hope that he'll find another mate eventually and have more cygnets.

As long as swans can fly, as long as springtime stirs the heart of both man and beast, well, H99, the swan, turned out to be no white-wilted wall flower.

Minnesota Wildlife Biologist: Low and behold this spring we had another pair with another marked male that were back here at Sellners Slough. Then H99 shows up and there was sort of a standoff and he claimed the territory and then he found himself a mate.

Minnesota Biologist: He must be a very good looking swan in the swan world because he never has trouble attracting a mate.

And there, back in Minnesota, our swan story ends. Soon after H99 courted a mate, the happy swan couple disappeared, never to be seen again.

Iowa Naturalist: H99 has touched a lot of lives. A lot of people have come to know and love him all the way from Texas to Iowa to Minnesota and Wisconsin.

They say fairy tales can come true. If so, maybe H99 and his lady have landed in Camelot...living happily ever after.

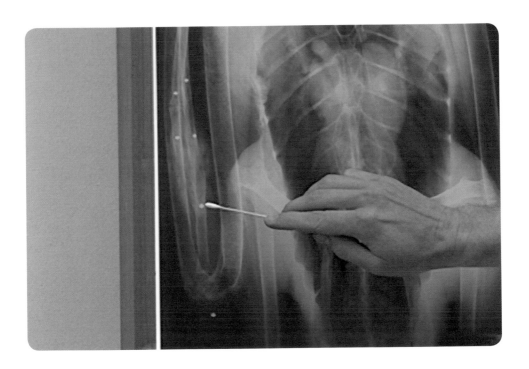

In the air or on the water, it's been said,
the bird appears like an armful of
white blossoms.

The Tamarack Tree

I remember the first time I saw a Tamarack tree and realized what it was. I had taken a college course in forestry — knowing the trees were part of the deal. Since then, the Tamarack has always been special to me. They tend to grow in ungodly places — they look like pine trees in summer. In winter, they look like dead trees. But in autumn, they glow like a rising sun. For that, we had to tell the Tamarack's story.

Maybe it glows simply to be noticed.

Ron's Narrative: It's a tree lovelier than poetry, to paraphrase Joyce Kilmer. It's also a tree most of us see without knowing what we see. Call it poetic justice for the Tamarack tree. It looks like an evergreen one day. Only to look days later like an autumn maple.

DNR Forester: It's an interesting tree. It's what we call a deciduous conifer. It breaks the rules. A Tamarack has 15 small needles in each cluster which is not unusual. But each fall those needles turn a bright fiery yellow and after they change colors they drop from the tree. A normal pine tree always keeps its needles green.

Along with two looks, the Tamarack tree even has two names. It's known as the American Larch to people who know trees. In the summer, people who don't know trees, figure the Tamarack is just another pine tree. It's green and has needles. The wood is strong but it grows in swamps. Maybe that's why you don't hear much about cabins or walls of Tamarack.

In early America, the pioneers thanked the Tamarack for lots of things. A concoction from the leaves and bark cured everything from piles to diarrhea to ulcers to something called dropsy, that is, when combined with spearmint, juniper berries and horseradish.

As the days of summer change to autumn, the Tamarack begins a slow transformation from plain green to brilliant yellow. You can say, it glows. Maybe it glows simply to be noticed.

Oh Tamarack would make a nice title to a song. Author James Boswell once noted, we must take our friends as they are. Perhaps the same should be said of the lowly Tamarack. After all, any tree that cures diarrhea is a friend of mine.

Winter Survival

If you've ever lived in a cold climate, you understand the agony of simply running from a warm house to a cold car. Even in warm clothes, it can give you the shivers. While I think of my own vulnerability to cold, the idea that song birds, deer and many other creatures face the cold 24 hours a day, 7 days a week, leaves me... well, shivering.

Survival is not a game in nature. It is a rule. But nature's creatures are well adapted to survival. Yet, every winter day brings or leads to death in the wild as winter is nature's bottleneck. We can't change that rule, either. But it makes for a good nature lesson.

During cold snaps, we add hats.
Heavy coats.
And winter boots.
But dainty chickadees
can't do that.
Deer neither.
Winter comes and Cardinals
are still wearing feathers more
fashionable on a beach somewhere.
Our dogs wear the same coat
winter or summer.
And the dog in your family also
needs a winter house.
So how do they survive when the
mercury falls?

Whitetail deer have learned to utilize the slightest edge, including infrared radiation beneath the branches of cedar, spruce and other evergreens. A whitetail never gets cold feet either — its hooves have few blood vessels or nerve endings. Deer also tend to move less in the dead of winter, conserving their stored energy.

All birds have the same advantage with their skinny, featureless legs. A numb toe is rare in the bird world. Starvation is rare, too. In winter storms, a wild turkey can go for two weeks without eating. However, small winter birds must eat almost every day. A chickadee can lose 10 percent of its body weight during one cold winter night.

We all know some animals sleep through some or all of winter.

Squirrels seem to have it both ways. If there's a January thaw, they're out and about. And during a cold snap, a squirrel sleeps until it's over.

Of all the wild critters, fish may have it the easiest over winter. Being cold blooded, they're comfortable at any depth.

Keep in mind, none of these creatures need or want our sympathy as we retreat to our warm houses. They are simply playing the earth's oldest game: survival of the fittest.

But my favorite game is survival of the smartest. Our Minnesota loons are all lollygagging in the warm waters of the Gulf of Mexico.

If we were smart, we'd be there with 'em.

With the Sandhills
PLATTE RIVER NEAR KEARNEY, NEBRASKA

Over the years I've been privileged to be present for spectacular sights. Everything from Victoria Falls in Africa to the living skies of Saskatchewan during the fall migration of waterfowl. Who would guess that on Nebraska's Platte River, on a sunny day in late march, my eyes would behold a work of nature that was unmatched by anything I'd ever seen. It was like a religious experience, the morning and evening flight of Sandhill Cranes. Who'd a thunk it.

Ron's Narrative: When sunrises and spring seasons come to Nebraska's Platte River, the moment is a sight to behold. Sandhill Cranes take to the air. Tens of thousands. Tens of thousands multiplied by ten. A sea of skinny legs and six foot wings. So many Sandhills, it's as if there's not enough sky to hold them all. The air itself is full, too. Full of the damndest sounds you've ever heard. And you can hear it miles away.

Doug Grann, CEO Wildlife Forever: They tell me that the Sandhill Crane has the loudest voice of all bird species and it has to do with their long necks. When you hear a hundred thousand of them at night – it is a sound from our past, it's a magical sound.

The Platte River is one of the most powerful places I've ever been in my life. I used to think that was reserved for the great wildernesses of Alaska, but when I slept on this riverbank, and woke up the next morning as a roar like a jet engine took off, I knew this was another powerful place in our great country.

Sandhills also are one of the oldest birds on earth, almost prehistoric, scientists say. They've been coming to the Platte River every spring for, not hundreds, but millions of years.

Paul Tebbel, Audubon's Rowe Sanctuary: In my mind what happens is the cranes are on their way north and they need a place to sit down. They need lots of energy to complete their migration. The Platte River is safety – it's wide, it's shallow, it's a perfect place for them to roost at night and the corn fields around provide almost all the food that they need.

From mid-February to early April, the migrating cranes pause along a short 80 mile stretch of the river near Kearney, Nebraska. Their next northbound stops are nesting grounds as far away as the arctic and Siberia.

Paul: In a given spring we'll get about 500,000 cranes through here. That's about 90 percent of the population.

For Sandhills, this is a serious business trip. The business of courtship dances to find a mate.

Paul: The dancing is an expression of several things, first it's always a part of the mating ritual between a male and female crane and it's a really important part. And it is really a stunning thing to watch. They are hopping in the air, they are flapping and bowing. It's a cool thing to see.

And watch it we do. Cranes attract upwards of 50,000 spectators a year to the banks of the Platte River.

Paul: We like to call this an awe experience. In other words this is a tremendous and appealing experience. It's a spectacle of nature.

But nature is always something we end up changing, especially rivers.

Doug: Certainly this migration is threatened mainly by the presence of man. These birds have been coming through here for 3 million years, and it is a tremendous story. But today there is a high demand for water on the prairie and when the levels are siphoned off for the irrigation of crops, it takes away water from the cranes.

The Platte River is like a refuge. At nightfall, cranes return to the Platte to roost in the sandy shallows to be safe from predators.

Doug: At the roost, when all those birds come thundering in, it moves you. It is part of mankind, something that our ancestors felt and the natives felt. It is something that we can still witness in this modern era.

And survive the cranes must. Without them, spring on the Platte just wouldn't be the same. And if somehow we lose this awesome spectacle of Sandhills – if our dawns and dusks on the Platte become silent, we would be possibly sadder than we've ever been before.

They have been coming to the Platte
River **every spring** for,
not hundreds, but **millions** of years.

A Day with Mike Blood
LAKE MINNETONKA, MINNESOTA

Until I met Mike Blood, he was a headline — a story in the 10 o'clock news on television. He'd been a cop who got shot by a bank robber. Years later, the name Mike Blood surfaced again. After a long struggle, his gunshot wounds had healed and he was leading a full life despite a few physical complications. I also learned something else about Mike Blood, he was an avid fisherman and he lived to fish. I knew then, Mike Blood's fishing story had to be our next fishing story.

Mike Blood: Here fishy, fishy.

Ron Schara: What do ya like about fishing?

Mike: It's relaxing – I don't think about other things.

Ron's Narrative: Since November of 2000, Mike Blood has had plenty of other things to think about.

Ron: Was there a time when you didn't think you would fish again?

Mike: Well, there was a time I didn't think I would live.

It happened at about 10:00 a.m. on a November morning in Edina, Minnesota.

Mike: I responded to a bank robbery call at 10 o'clock in the morning at a bank on France Avenue. I pulled into the parking lot and went about 50 feet and saw a car facing out with no plates. I peeked in and there was a bunch of guns and ammo sitting on the front seat. As I was backing up, he popped up between two cars right next to my squad car's passenger door. When I turned my head and he realized I saw him, he pulled off the first shot from right outside the passenger window. That one went through my hips.

Could be decent size fish here – I can still feel him thumping. He's staying down pretty good.

Ron: What is it?

Mike: A bass.

Ron: Ohh it's a big bass. Good catch Mike.

Mike: The bank robber circled to the front spraying bullets at me as he went. One of them went through the back window and broke the window into a lot of little pieces that hit my leg. That's why the entry wound is 6 inches across. I fell forward. I couldn't do anything, so I played dead stopped breathing and just laid face down. He came around to the back of the squad about 8 feet behind me and put two more in my lower back.

The next day police officer Mike Blood was making the kind of headlines every cop fears.

Mike: The four doctors who had worked on me told me they thought I was going to die. It was a miracle I was alive.

It's also a miracle that continues. Mike Blood is casting again, catching again and...reflecting again.

Ron: Would you be a cop again if you were starting over?

Mike: Yes, starting over with a new body. But yes, I found it to be fulfilling work.

Despite bullet scars, Blood's original body still works wonders in the water. One of his favorite pursuits is snorkeling to spear carp on Lake Minnetonka.

Mike: I've done it just about every year. As a matter of fact, I've done it every year other than the year I was pretty badly injured. Once I knew I was going to live, I had my mind set that I would be able to swim and fish.

Mike's struggle to regain his life hasn't been a lonely one. He's been recognized for his valor and remembered as a home town hero.

Sherry, Mike's Wife: I try not to put the handicap as the primary problem. It's a problem we have to deal with but we're going to go out and we're going to go fishing. We're going to go snorkeling and we're just going to try to do things as normally as we can.

Today Mike and Sherry willingly share with others their message of hope in desperate times.

Mike: I appreciate my life a lot more. I don't care as much about what the Vikings did last Sunday. I care more about my friends and my family. There was one major thing that saved me and that was God – It's a miracle that I'm here.

So, Mike Blood the miracle, keeps casting for fish or swimming with 'em. While the bad guy in this story is gone, killed in a shoot-out with other cops.

Mike: I've moved on with life. I'm really happy to be here, believe me.

Post Script: Mike continues an active life and is still fishing!

The **four doctors** who had
worked on me told me they thought
I was going to die.
It was a **miracle I was alive.**

Al Maas, Guide Extraordinaire
LEECH LAKE, MINNESOTA

Minnesota is blessed with a boatload of colorful fishing guides. One of the most colorful is a fella named Al Maas. His is quite a story and as comfortable as an old shoe. Al brings to Minnesota's outdoor scene a sense of history, of intellect, of tragedy and unabashed love. I also caught the largest muskie of my life while sharing a boat with Al. The downside was...no cameraman was there to record it. We do have pictures, however. And we did the Al Maas story without landing a muskie...and nobody noticed.

Ron's Narrative: It's another day on Minnesota's Leech Lake. And another day on the job for one of Minnesota's best known muskie fishing guides. His name? Al Maas.

Al Maas: Well, let's pop one for old time's sake.

He's been 40 years a muskie guide, 40 years of casting for the improbable catch.

Al: Give it time here, see what happens.

Ron Schara: You probably have most of these fishes named don't ya?

Al: There he is! Oh, I missed him – I missed him! Did he hit the lure? Yeah. There was that big fish Ron. Oh no! I heard that splash.

Ron: That's the way it goes...I've been there before.

Al: That sucks (laughs) I've been there before too. She hit the lure and you get one crack. She moved a lot of water, a huge fish. Like I said, I knew she was 40 pounds. I've seen her so many times.

So goes the life and times of Al Maas, a man of many faces.

Al: You have to have a desire and you have to have success or you're not going to be doing this. You have to get rewards fast or you're not going back to do it.

I've lucked out and I caught some big fish in my days. Once you catch one, you're hooked and you know that.

If he sounds like an old coach and teacher, it is because he once was. Al Maas once led the 1968 Walker, Minnesota football team to an undefeated season. Now retired from teaching, Al and his wife Dianne chose to stay close to the shores of Leech Lake.

Al: I decided a long time ago if I didn't like fishing, I'd have a very boring life, so we all – our whole family loves fishing and we love the outdoors.

In 1984 their love of the outdoors and Leech Lake was severely tested when two sons, Chuck and Douglas, drowned in a wind storm while duck hunting on the big lake.

Al: Like you say, you don't know what the day will bring. Within 24 hours when I knew what had happened I said ok, we have several options, but this is the route we're going to go. Our boys loved the outdoors, my wife knew that and my daughter knew that, so we continued to pursue what they had enjoyed all their life and we don't regret one bit of it.

For Al, guiding on Leech Lake became his therapy.

Al: It's a vast body of water which can keep you very entertained because you can go from one species of fish to the next very easily. It's a lake where you can always get into protected waters – it has beautiful, pristine water, very clear.

You know of the thousands of people that I've guided, I've probably only had one bad client in all the years – its been great. And watching people catch their first fish, especially a muskie, is really rewarding to me.

Rewarding to me was catching the largest muskie of my life, a 49-incher, with Al as the guide.

Al: I remember you that day.

Ron: My eyes were wide, even though it was raining.

When he isn't guiding, Al is tinkering with lure designs, new ways to fool an old adversary – the muskie.

Al: These are some we're working on now...this is called a dinner bell.

Meanwhile back on the lake, Al and I continued in search of a hungry muskie. It's just a matter of finding the right one.

Al: Well, the difference is at least I know they're here.

A few casts later, the guide was right again.

Al: Here he comes! Follow the lure – come behind it, keep him coming Ron. C'mon hit it...oh, dammit...dang, ohhhh...we're having a good one here...that was a good fish. He boiled it on there, never touched the lure – never touched it.

After 40 years of guiding, Al Maas understands the mystique of muskies.

Ron: You get to see a lot of people catch the fish of a lifetime.

Al: That part is true, that's what it's all about. Their eyes get about 4 feet wide and they want the fish in the boat right now. I get such a kick out of that.

Enough of a kick to do it all again day after day.

I decided a long time ago
**if I didn't
like fishing,**

I'd have a
very boring
life.

All About Dick Beardsley
DETROIT LAKES, MINNESOTA

If anybody made running famous in Minnesota, it was a guy named Dick Beardsley. He became synonymous with pushing one's body to the brink under the guise of marathons. Dick also was the perfect story. A city boy with a shy manner who was never comfortable under the glare of attention. When we caught up with Dick, his life had, had more ups and downs than a bicycle pedal. His competitive running career was long over and his days in the headlines were long gone. The Dick Beardsley we found had chosen a new path of life that included days spent fishing as a paid guide. While he no longer ran for the glory, he still ran a few miles every morning before daylight and before his next fishing trip.

Ron's Narrative: In his race through life, Dick Beardsley, is floating along these days at a different pace. On the streets of Detroit Lakes, Minnesota, where Beardsley calls home today he's known as a summer fishing guide. And when he's not fishing, he's a radio DJ for local country station, KDLM. The other Dick Beardsley, the one America knew, is not around much anymore. The Dick Beardsley, who once dominated the headlines as a world class runner, is a life now relegated to old newspaper clippings.

Dick Beardsley: The Boston papers dubbed me "the country bumpkin from Minnesota" and I kinda got a kick out of it. I think it was because, just being from Minnesota – my mannerisms, and sayings like "jeepers," "you betcha" and "cotton-pickin" – they just got the biggest kick out of that.

The day fans of the Boston Marathon learned to adore the country bumpkin, was the day Beardsley pushed world record holder Alberto Salazar to a photo finish in the marathon of marathons.

Dick: It was unbelievable. It was a race I'll never forget, even though it was over 20 years ago. It's like it happened yesterday in my mind.

Now at this point, we're about 100 meters to go, but I thought about two mistakes I made. One: I didn't know where the finish line was. And secondly, when I caught up to Salazar, I was dead, but I had momentum going and I should have just used it to fly by him but instead I caught up to him and I sat back for just a moment to catch my breath, and he took off. Then I took off behind him, and that's how the race finished. We were fortunate – both of us broke the American record that day and the course record, but he ran 2 hours, 8 minutes and 51 seconds, I ran 2 hours 8 minutes and 53 seconds. So, two seconds separated us at the very end, but I wouldn't trade it for a million dollars.

Minnesota's most famous runner was in the big leagues now, a goal he'd had since boyhood.

Dick: I started running as a junior in high school – the fall of my junior year because I was so shy with girls. I just could not ask a girl out for a date, and I would see my buddies wearing their Wayzata letter jackets, and they always had girls hanging around 'em. So, I went out for football, believe it or not, trying to win a letter jacket, and that lasted about 45 and a half minutes, I thought "there's no girl worth getting beat up like this for!" And then a friend of mine said "you outta come out for cross country running." And I did! Oh, the confidence! When I got my letter jacket, I actually asked a girl – a cheerleader – out to the homecoming dance. That date didn't last much longer than my football career, but it was a start, you know?

It was the start of Dick's running fame that spread from Grandma's Marathon to the London Marathon and finally to Boston in the time of two hours and nine minutes.

Dick: It was the best race and the hardest race, and I think if Alberto Salazar was here, he'd tell you the same thing. I left something on the race course that day, and he did too.

Dick Beardsley's race through life also took a strange turn. While he hoped for a running comeback, misfortune struck. Over a period of several years, Beardsley was involved in three separate but severe accidents.

Dick: Well, you know, I never asked God why this is happening to me. I just figured it happened, and you just gotta get on with things.

I'm still alive, there must be a good reason for that. Then I got hit by a truck, was back in the hospital, and ended up having to have a major back surgery. And somehow, I ended up addicted to pain killers.

Beardsley became so addicted, he began to illegally write his own prescriptions.

Dick: And then finally on September 30 of 1996, I went into the Wal-Mart store in Moorhead, where I had gone many times before, and I had three fake prescriptions and I gave 'em to the gal, and she said "that'll be about ten minutes." And I turned to the pharmacist, who I had become friends with, he was an avid fisherman, waiting for him to say "Dick, how's fishing been?" and he never said a word. He stopped counting his pills, and...

Beardsley's race for drugs was over and his race for drug treatment was just beginning.

Dick: When all of a sudden this broke, it was on national news, it was in papers – everywhere all over the country – and our son Andy was in like the fifth or sixth grade at the time, and all the kids at school said "ooh, your dad's dealing cocaine."

I'm a very positive person, but that's the lowest I've ever been. I was. I mean, I'll be honest with you, I don't get to church every Sunday, but every morning, when I'm out doing my walk or doing my run, I have my little one-on-one with God.

And it is without a doubt the hardest thing I've had to try to overcome. And it will be something I will have to continue to work at every single day for the rest of my life.

Today, Dick Beardsley has a new addiction – fishing.

Dick: Just being out in the boat, there were times that it helped a lot.

Fishing Friend: He's a person that doesn't quit. He has an eternal sunny disposition, and he just doesn't quit. He's a great guy to be around and he loves to fish! He's out fishing as often as he can.

Before his fishing trips, Dick Beardsley, now more than 50, still runs every morning. And every step is positive.

Dick: Well, you gotta be. Its helped me through a lot of nasty stuff. And I'll tell you this, the last six and a half years of my life have without question been the best six and a half years that I've had.

At last, maybe the rough miles are behind him.

Minnesota's most famous runner

was in the big leagues now,

a goal he'd had since boyhood.

Don "El Gia"
MAZATLAN, MEXICO

I first met Don McFarland about 35 years ago at a Ducks Unlimited banquet in Minneapolis. Don was a flamboyant soul who loved a good laugh, a good drink and a good fish on the line. He was an adventuring soul which may explain why my next meeting with Don was in Mazatlan, Mexico in the year 1970, as I recall. Don was launching a fishing tournament for Minnesota tourists coming to Mexico and he thought the idea would make great reading in the old Minneapolis Tribune. My editors agreed. Since that day, I became a member of the Don McFarland fan club. He might have been the life of the party in ol' Mexico but he also was a generous soul to Mexicans less fortunate than he and his wife, Patti. Over the years, Don and Patti had given thousands of dollars to help Mazatlan schools and orphanages. This was a Minnesota fishing story that needed to be told.

Ron's Narrative: A moment of truth for any angler. When yellow finned tuna below the sea go on a feeding rampage joined above by dolphins.

Don McFarland: Give it a go guys – ha, ha. There's one right here – who wants to fight a fish. This is it, this is what it is all about.

To Don, The Guide, what it's really all about is living life with gusto. Gusto in a fishing boat. Gusto in all you do. Meet Don McFarland. To his friends in Mazatlan, Mexico, he is Don "El Gia" – Don The Guide.

More than three decades ago, Don McFarland discovered the key to life his way. It began with a story about deep sea fishing in the pacific off the shores of Mazatlan.

Don: So I flew down here to Mazatlan – went fishing and caught 9 sailfish and 2 dorados in 4 hours and I was hooked. This place is paradise.

To live in paradise, Don The Guide and entrepreneur soon had Minneapolis to Mazatlan charter flights filled, not with tourists, but with anglers like himself.

Don: I didn't have a clue (laughter) of pretty much everything I was doing, but I put up a great front and nobody knew that I didn't have a clue.

Patti McFarland, Wife: He came home the first time with pictures saying we were going to Mazatlan and I was nervous...Very nervous. Until I walked out of the Hotel Playa and saw the beach – it was the most beautiful thing I had laid my eyes on.

Mazatlan also was an inviting destination to winter weary Minnesotans. It has the largest shrimp fleet in all of Mexico, sunny beaches and colorful Mexican cultural events. In addition to great night clubs with wild and crazy names. So begins McFarland's travel tours to Mazatlan.

Don: We went into yearly trips from then on and I went into the full service charter business. Four years later, we were running 13 jets a year full of tourists.

Life was good. Don and wife Patti spent their winters with tourists in Mazatlan and their summers in Brainerd helping tourists meet Paul Bunyan himself. While the years and the Mexican trips went by, Don "El Gia" never lost his passion for big game fishing off the waters of Mazatlan.

Don: This is the Pacific, you head out of here and your next stop is Hawaii. We go out after marlin or sailfish or tarpon – big fish, but tuna is what we are really looking for because there are a lot of them.

And when you find the tuna you find the ocean's version of the chain of life. Birds, dolphins and tuna all feeding in unison.

Don: There's one on!

It was a fishing moment that wouldn't end.

Ron Schara: My goodness, you are never ready for the strength.

Don: Aren't they beautiful? You never get tired of watching that phenomenon, it's the web of life right in front of you. With the tuna eating, and the dolphins eating the tuna and the birds on top eating what all the others have missed. This will go on for an hour or more.

And when the day ends, Don heads to port with plenty of tuna flags flying in the breeze. Yet, fishing is not the whole story about the good life of Don "El Gia."

Don: We added on to this orphanage a number of years ago. That is for babies – a little room in there. And around the corner is an infirmary. Over there, we built a park for kids to play in.

This orphanage on the outskirts of Mazatlan would not exist if it wasn't for Don and Patti McFarland.

Don: When we built the hotel I said I want to do something for the city of Mazatlan – they said well, you ought to go out and help the "ciudad los ninos" (city of children).

One improvement the McFarland's paid for was running water.

Don: None of the kids out here are for adoption – they were dropped off by their parents and they may come back to get them. While they are here, they are one big happy family but you can't adopt them.

Across town, the McFarland's have supported another cause. It's a grade school that was getting crowded.

Don: The girls in 6th grade were going to have to go to another school because they didn't have any more space and I said what if I build a couple rooms? So, that's what I did.

School Official: I think it means a lot – especially to some of the older ones. Some of them have told me that since the McFarland's have been coming for so many years that Christmas time is a special time for them because that is when they know that the McFarland's will be bringing them gifts.

So you can see, Don "El Gia," is more than a fishing guide. In the rough seas of life, he hopes to bring what he has known, some calm, happiness, and good luck.

Patti: Don is unique and unstoppable. There are no walls for Don McFarland. He'll go thru them, over them, under them and around them – there are no walls. My favorite phrase is Frank Sinatra's "I did it my way." To me that describes him perfectly.

This orphanage on the outskirts of Mazatlan

would not exist

if it wasn't for

Don and Patti McFarland.

Feather Painter

When I first heard about Lynda Wood and the special art that she practiced, I knew we had to tell her story. What I didn't know was the **impact her story would have** on our Minnesota Bound viewers. To this day, we've had **more inquiries** about Lynda and her art form **than almost any other story** we've done. Indeed, she has a **special artistic gift**.

Ron's Narrative: Lynda Wood paints a different picture.

Lynda Wood: If it was going to be wildlife, I guess it would have to be a wolf. The wolves, the eagles, and the deer are my 3 favorite things to paint. And all of them are well, light as a feather.

I started doing feather paintings in 1994. The first one I did was the half face of a wolf on a feather and from there we just decided it was maybe a good thing to try.

Now her easel may hold half a wing's worth.

Lynda: This is a five feather arrangement of turkey feathers and it's a little bit more involved than previous ones I've done. I've got more trees on there and I think the trees are even harder to do than the feathers or eagles themselves.

They take the longest and yeah, I guess they are the hardest ones to do because I start with the middle feather here and then lay the feathers down on top of it and hot glue each one so they all lay right together. It's a little bit more involved than just doing a single feather.

As good artists do, Lynda Wood makes her feather art look so easy.

Lynda: When I was in grade school I used to get in trouble for doodling and drawing a lot when I was supposed to be doing other things. I've always had an interest in doing some kind of drawing or painting. I think the most difficult part is there are so many layers that have to be worked with and you have to work with the direction the feather is going.

And, Lynda insists, any bird on a feather oughta look real enough to fly away.

Lynda: The most important part is the eyes of the animals – to give them life the eyes have to look just right. And working on feathers you're working much smaller than you would for an ordinary painting, so it's quite tricky to keep them looking right.

Just as every feather is a one-of-a-kind, so are Lynda's paintings.

Lynda: A lot of people will stand there and be looking at the pictures and ask, did you paint these? Is it air brushed? Is it screen printed? That's why I sit at the shows and paint, so that they know that it's not mass produced.

I have paintings from coast to coast, from Germany to Sweden.

You could say, Lynda Wood's artwork – painting on a feather – really is taking off.

The most important part is the eyes.

Fishing with the President
RUM RIVER, MINNESOTA

In my business, you hear lots of **rumors and stuff.** One of the most interesting rumors to cross my desk was about Robert Bruininks, the President of the University of Minnesota. Somebody said **he's a fisherman.** Well, we had to find out. After many attempts to schedule a fishing trip, we finally succeeded and the president came to my backyard and we took a float trip down the Rum River. Besides fodder for the mind, the president also showed a **good sense of humor** when his fishing outfit, a very expensive rod and reel, accidentally went overboard in the river never to be seen again. I felt awful. But when a president laughs, one should **laugh with him.** So...I did.

Robert Bruininks, University of Minnesota President: I've always had a life long interest in the outdoors.

Ron's Narrative: Floatin' and fishin' on Minnesota's Rum River – this angler's mind of higher learning gets it right.

Robert: A slow day on the river is always better than any day at the office.

So says the man who sits in one of Minnesota's highest offices. U of M President Robert Bruininks. A gopher booster since 1968, Bruinink was named president several years ago. Among his qualifications – a passion for fishing.

Robert: I started fishing as a small boy, we'd get on our bikes and go to a lake. I find fishing is one of the ways to get away the daily stress of the job. It's a good way to unwind.

As we drifted, Bruinink's academic mind took note of society's failures at stabilizing river banks and farmland. The president believes the U of M can be a leader in being smarter stewards of the land.

Robert: We think the University of Minnesota with some prudent investments can be a leader and world center for fresh water research and wild life and natural resources research.

You could say this bass fishing trip was for scientific purposes. Will a smallmouth bass eat a fake frog?

Robert: Oh my, hold still…it's a big bass! That's a good fish, oh yeah…a big fish. Go Gophers!

Cheering about a big catch is nothing new for the U of M president. His own really big fish shares his office.

Robert: This is my friend Wilma – caught in 1989, she's 17 pounds 6 ounces.

Wilma also is only two ounces shy of Minnesota's record walleye. While he's proud of his fish, Bruinink is more proud of his campus.

Robert: Being here keeps you young and it keeps you on your toes. You are always challenged to defend your views – it's a very exciting place to be.

Students know him, too.

Robert: (Talking to a student) We were fishing on the Rum River and Schara caught a huge fish on the trip.

Robert: I am most proud that this University is one of the top 5 public research Universities in the United States – based on measured productivity.

A college president must have patience and fishing teaches that.

Robert: Being the president is not a job, it's a calling.

Just like catching a fish.

Ron Schara: Wow…c'mom Bob man handle him, all right, all right, now that's a fish! That's a big fish…ha, ha.

This president gets an "A" in fishing class.

Being the president is **not a job,**
it's a calling.

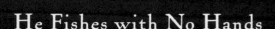

He Fishes with No Hands

I first learned about Steve Larson when somebody saw him fishing in a boat on Opening Day of Minnesota's walleye season. Steve was noticeable because he was the only angler out there who was fishing **with his feet instead of his hands.** The day we filmed Steve doing his thing I was privileged to share the boat with him. You could feel his **determination** to go fishing and **have fun doing it.** Over the years I've had many enjoyable fishing partners, but nobody matches Steve for angling inspiration.

Ron's Narrative: When Steve Larson goes fishing he needs not a helping hand. His feet are his hands. His feet steer the outboard and scoop the minnows. His feet even bait his hook.

Steve Larson: This was the crowning achievement of my fishing – being able to pick up a small crappie minnow without crushing it.

That's just the start of this fishing story. It also wouldn't be stretching the truth to say Steve Larson is an extraordinary fishing partner.

Steve: I was born without arms. A congenital birth defect. There was really no known reason for it and I just naturally have adapted to the use of my feet. Thank goodness I had parents, older brothers and grandparents that loved me for who I was and didn't think it was unclean to use my feet or anything like that – it was just the natural process.

Beyond his missing arms, Steve is exactly what he wants to be, an ordinary guy.

Steve: I have a family. I have children. I have a great career. I've got this beautiful home here and we are able to contribute meaningfully to our community.

Julie Jo Larson, Wife: Sometimes I take for granted what he does. Sometimes we'll go bowling or golfing or something and I'll forget and he'll say hon, can I have my ball please or can you get that for me or something like that.

And what Steve does with his legs, his feet and his toes is like, well, handy.

Steve: I'm right footed just as you would have a dominant hand I have a dominant foot.

And his feet have very talented toes.

Steve: I can cook and I can wash the dishes – unfortunately. I changed all 3 of my children's diapers – another skill I did not want to learn but my wife didn't give me any choice. So there are a number of things I can't do, but in terms of my independence, being able to drive a car, being able to write, being able to type, and operate a computer – all of those things I'm able to do – and efficiently.

Yet it's in a fishing boat where Steve's determination is tested to the limits.

Steve: You know the ability to learn to put a crappie minnow on a small 32 ounce jig head with your feet is a struggle. It's still a struggle tying those knots. But I've got the ability to catch muskie and lake trout, crappie and grayling. And I've caught all those fish and I'm pretty proud of that.

While Steve drove the outboard with feet, he pulled up to a fishing spot and, with his feet, dropped the anchor, picked up a fishing rod, opened the reel bail and made a cast.

An avid fisherman, Steve's feet seem to dance in the boat. Especially when something is on the end of the line. To hold the rod, he slips his right foot into a sandal that is connected to the top of the rod handle. His left foot is used to turn the reel handle when its time to pull in a fish.

Steve: Little bass or is it a big bluegill? It's a bluegill – nice one. There we go.

Nice fish, yes. But watching him cast and reel. Watching him pick up a tiny minnow with his toes and put the bait on the hook. Watching him unhook a pan fish with his toes. Watching him pick up his fish with his toes. Watching him raise his leg to show off his catch. Watching him smile and deftly toss his fish back into the lake.

You cannot fish with Steve without learning a special fishing lesson. You discover that it's not only the catching that counts. You learn that being out there on the water is important. You learn that just being able to go fishing is a precious gift.

Lastly, you realize that fishing with an inspiration is a day you'll never forget.

Steve is **exactly** what he wants to be, **an ordinary guy.**

Maker of Birch Bark Canoes
BIG FORK RIVER, MINNESOTA

If life is full of surprises, the same can be said of our Minnesota Bound expeditions. One day we stopped and walked into an old shed with a weathered name on the front. It didn't look like much. But the surprise was inside. Years before, we discovered, Charles Kuralt had walked through the same doors and undoubtedly found the same surprise. Kuralt was there to do a story on a maker of birch bark canoes. I did the same story a generation later.

Ron's Narrative: This enterprise known as Bill Hafeman's boat works was founded 1921 and is still thriving. If time ever stands still it might be inside. Birch bark canoes are made here. Made by hand. Just as they were 500 years ago.

Ray Boessel: This is the birch bark. These pieces are all cut to shape.

Canoe maker Ray Boessel took over the business in 1981 a few years before Bill Hafeman, his mentor and his wife's grandfather, passed away.

Ray: My wife taught me on the first two I made and after that I worked three years for Bill until he took early retirement at age 85. But nothing else about birch bark canoes has changed much.

It takes a lot of looking to find the right bark you need for a canoe. Birch bark is really amazing stuff. It's a lot stronger than what it looks like.

To sew the birch bark pieces together, Boessel gathers roots from spruce trees in nearby swamps and keeps them wet in the Big Fork River, his backyard testing grounds.

Ray: I kinda like digging roots in the swamp – I'm kinda a strange person I guess. The mosquitoes don't normally bother you in the swamp if you pick roots fast enough – they think you are crazy.

In an average year, Ray Boessel will make about 15 canoes, each selling for more than $2,000.

Ray: It'll take eight hours of stripping and splitting the roots to make 500 feet of bindings, enough to finish a 16-foot canoe.

And every canoe is an original. Its parts and pieces formed by hand-tools older than the canoe builder, himself.

Ray: This cedar log is split and split again. What I have to get down to first is how wide I want my ribs. So, I keep splitting into pie shapes for thickness that way.

Ray says he works about 80 hours to complete a canoe. It's a slow task that looks more like a magical act.

Ray: I mostly just eyeball everything. That's all Indians had to begin with. They didn't have Stanley rulers and micrometers and stuff like that. You just kinda get to know where it looks right and where a canoe rib ought to be. It's just that easy.

Eventually all of the assembled parts, the bark, the cedar ribs and cedar gunwales are lashed together with spruce roots. And canoe number 205 is about to come off the assembly line.

Ray: This is what holds the whole canoe together, the roots. There's no nails or glue whatsoever.

Ray even offers a guarantee. If the roots ever break, he'll redo the bindings for nothing.

Ray: Nothing to it. We've got a little bit of advantage over what the natives had because of my tools. But Indians had an advantage in the quality of materials they had to work with.

When the last root is tied, Ray takes each canoe for a test paddle in the river next door.

Ray: I've had guys come in and want me to mass produce them and they'd sell 'em for me. But I don't want to do that.

When you make birch bark canoes and live history every day, fame and fortune is not in the company plan.

Ray: This way I make enough to make a living for my family and that keeps me happy.

And a river to paddle away.

Meet the Walker

Over the television seasons, we've met top anglers, trick shooters and arctic explorers who were driven beyond the endurance of most humans. Each had a story to tell. Then, one day we met John Hamper. He didn't fish. He didn't shoot. He traveled some, but never across an ice pack. Yet, John had a unique story to tell, too. He was a walker. Yes, he liked to walk. Although, that's probably an understatement.

Ron's Narrative: His passion is one step at a time, one foot following the other... season after season.

John Hamper, The Walker: In winter it's tougher, there's the wind chill on your skin.

And into spring, followed by summer. And when the leaves fall – so do his footsteps still with a song in his walking heart.

Ron Schara: What kind of speed do you walk at?

John: (taking off) Kind of like this.

Meet Minnesota's Walker. Walker with a capitol W.

John: I'm the Minnesota State Champion and I'm the most prolific Volksmarcher in Minnesota.

You won't find John Hamper's name in Minnesota's Sports Hall of Fame or the amazing distances he's walked.

John: So far I've walked 42,750 miles. That's the equivalent of one time around the world at the equator, from North Pole to South Pole and a double crossing of the USA.

You heard right. Miles. 42,750 in the last 22 years. From Minnesota to as far away as Volksmarches in Europe.

John: One time I walked 68 miles in 20 hours and 5 minutes. That's two marathons back to back plus 16 miles.

So how, pray tell, does one get hooked on something most Americans like to avoid? Walking anywhere.

John: Sometimes I think about life situations, sometimes I just enjoy the scenery. Every once in a while I meet a person or a pretty scene so I slow down to take it in.

A former resident of Melrose, Minnesota, the Walker says he stumbled on his passion during a hitch in the U.S. Air Force in Germany.

John: I had a good time so it's something I wanted to do on a regular basis. In my prime I could do 62 miles each weekend. My one year record was 3,700 miles.

Ron: I can't even imagine how far that is.

The Walker says when you don't ride you notice things. This Minneapolis street – 15th and Madison, has four churches in one block. John says that's a record. And despite a few blisters, the Walker says he sees no end in sight to his footsteps.

John: It's very healthy. It gives me a reason to go out and see the world and travel to places most folks can only read about. I enjoy the sense of accomplishment and making the milestones.

The Walker's new goal? Only 20,000 more miles to go.

In my prime I could do
62 miles each weekend.
My one year record was 3,700 miles.

Arnie the Wood Duck Man

One day wildlife artist David Maas told me about a special friend. His name was Arnie. Arnie has wood duck boxes pasted all over his house, David said. It sounded like a story. How wonderful a story I was about to discover.

Ron's Narrative: It's Beethoven night with the Mankato symphony. Dianne Pope conducting.

And there, looking quite dapper in the second violin section is, 72 year-old, Arnold Krueger, playing as he has for a half century.

Dianne Pope, Conductor: Arnie is wonderfully gifted musically – a great violinist and an absolute professional.

Arnie Krueger: When I'm playing I try not to think of anything else outside of the music, especially if I'm thinking about ducks.

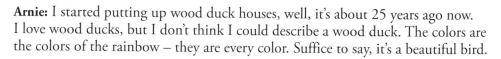

What's this? Beethoven's 9th symphony mixed with web-footed ducks? Welcome to the world of Arnie Krueger.

Arnie: I started putting up wood duck houses, well, it's about 25 years ago now. I love wood ducks, but I don't think I could describe a wood duck. The colors are the colors of the rainbow – they are every color. Suffice to say, it's a beautiful bird.

So beautiful that Arnie has wood duck boxes hanging everywhere. In the trees. On his garage. On his house. Even under the TV satellite dish.

Arnie: I just thought it would be fun to put one close so I could watch and they loved it.

Ron Schara: Now your house is covered.

Arnie: I know it, I know it. My wood duck houses have more wood than the house (laughter).

In Arnie's world, each duck house is numbered. And once a week in nesting season, Arnie checks to see who's at home.

Arnie: I keep track of each house. How many eggs are in the house. If it's marked with yellow that means the mother duck is in there and she's incubating the eggs.

Arnie peeks into house number 41.

Arnie: She's looking right at me – she may have little ones under her. I don't want to disturb her. One thing I know – it doesn't bother the ducks at all if you handle their eggs. Some people think if you touch an egg a hen won't come back, but I haven't found that to be true at all.

Arnold says he'll stop adding wood duck houses when he reaches 50 boxes. That's the same number of years he's taught music. He's also been married for 50 years – to Earlys, his piano playing sweetheart.

Arnie: When we play music together she knows what direction I'm going to go and I know which direction she's gonna go.

And they both know the high note at the dinner table.

Arnie: I cooked two ducks for dinner. One is a mallard and one is a wood duck. A lot of things you eat you love. I like wood ducks and I like to eat wood ducks.

Arnold's small farm with a number of small ponds has been developed for ducks of all kinds.

Arnie: I think that musicians have to be sensitive people and to be a good outdoorsman, you have to be sensitive too, sensitive to wildlife and the world around you.

Beethoven's notes may pour from Arnie's violin, but long ago he composed his own song of life.

Arnie: There are three important things in my life, first I say my wife and family, then music, then ducks.

Arnie is a lucky duck.

To be a good outdoorsman,
you have to be **sensitive** to wildlife
and the **world around you.**

Dog Man Extraordinaire
OAK RIDGE KENNELS, NORTHFIELD, MINNESOTA

If there was ever a television story on Minnesota Bound that made sense, it's the story about **pro dog trainer**, Tom Dokken. Long before my television career began, my labs were graduates of Tom's Oak Ridge Kennels in Northfield, Minnesota. What I liked about Tom's training techniques was this: When you bring Tom a happy dog to train — what you get back is a **trained happy dog**. My first memory of Tom Dokken and his Labradors was **more pandemonium than happiness**, however.

Years ago, the Northwest Sportshow at the Minneapolis Convention Center also included a daily stage show with circus acts, dog acts and the like. Sportshow producer Phil and Dave Perkins hired me to open the stage show with a little local outdoor fun and to introduce the Star Spangled Banner. One year I decided my "act" would include live wild turkeys. The birds were my pets and I had conditioned them to sit on a portable tree branch. Back then, most Minnesotans had never seen wild turkeys. So, I would show off the birds, talk about them and – for my closing performance – I would pick up a bird and have it fly back to the portable tree branch. Despite their size, wild turkeys are excellent flyers.

Show after show, the turkeys performed perfectly. But one night, as I let the turkey loose to fly, it apparently was blinded by the spotlights. The big bird missed the tree branch and landed awkwardly on the slippery stage. That would have been fine, except the next act was Tom Dokken and his trained Labs. One of the Labs happened to see the flapping wings hit the stage and assumed a retrieve was in order. As I rushed to pick up my startled turkey, a streaking Lab pounced on the bird. My stage act had turned to chaos. Feathers flew and I was trying to rescue my startled turkey and Tom Dokken was racing to the stage to retrieve his retriever. The crowd roared with delight. When the chaos ended, my turkey was fine and Tom's Lab was backstage again. I introduced the national anthem and the main show went on. Tom and I? We've been great friends ever since.

Ron's Narrative: Man's best friend – if you really want to know the truth – didn't happen by accident.

Tom Dokken: A lot of people's conception of dog training – and we hear this all the time when we are talking to people on the road is – "I'd love to be a dog trainer because you go out and have fun and play with dogs all day long." But the reality of the job is that it's a 24 hour a day commitment.

Meet Tom Dokken. Dog trainer 24 hours a day now for more than 25 years. And most of his canine students arrive at Oak Ridge Kennels dumber than a leash.

Tom: On the first day coming in for training we see immediately when the dog gets out of the car what our challenge is. We know in the first 15 seconds.

Sometimes it's not the dog who needs the most training.

Tom: We can have a dog that is listening fantastically to us as far as the dog trainers are concerned, but if the owners don't know how to handle the dog and how to keep it working properly, you are not going to be happy when the dog goes home.

Frankly, the life of a professional dog trainer doesn't sound like much doggone fun.

Tom: It's like the postal service – regardless of what the weather is the mail must go out – so does dog training. So, when it is 30 below in the middle of the winter time – we're out. And when it is 96 degrees and humidity is high – you are out dog training.

Not to mention cleaning dog kennels and crap like that, if you know what I mean. Yet Tom Dokken wouldn't have it any other way.

Tom: The only reason that you are in this business is because you like dogs and in my case I like all animals. And for the people who come work for us at Oak Ridge Kennels, their love of the dogs is number one – from there the training is just a secondary occupation and when you are in a job that you love, it shows.

It shows in the dogs. Raven, the television star, learned her smarts here. And now her coach has become a television celebrity.

Tom: When you are passionate about dog training, and are passionate about the animals – it's great to be able to help somebody over the TV that has a problem. We do a lot of training tips and we hear back from people all the time. When we are around the country and somebody says – "I've seen the training tip about such and such, I tried it and it worked" – It's gratifying. How else can you do that but on TV?

The big part of the job that is so rewarding is that you can see a dog come in with no training or knowledge at all and send him home trained – that's the gratification of the job.

So, if you are going to think about getting in the dog training business – what you really have to do is be committed and put the time in to learn it. For hunting dog training, there really isn't a school out there that you can go to. You are going to have to serve an apprenticeship. A dog trainer can go any place in the United States or any where in the world and find a job because it is a hand-crafted profession.

The result – from Tom Dokken – is a smarter dog – but still a happy one.

The only reason that you are
in this business is because **you like dogs**
and in my case
I like all animals.

Miracle in Town
MOUNTAIN IRON, MINNESOTA

The **power of the human spirit** never fails to impress us. In many ways, those of us whose lives are less difficult oddly **find strength** through the stories of those less fortunate. This story is about a young man who wasn't going to be denied from an outdoor dream he **wouldn't quit dreaming.**

Ron's Narrative: If you're looking for a miracle, there's one that leaves this garage almost every day. It happens when Terry Knuti drives away on the streets of the small mining town of Mountain Iron, Minnesota. And when he returns home, well his father and mother see that as a miracle, too.

Terry's Mother: Back on August 5th of 1981 Terry was run over – he and his sister Kelly. Terry was 4 years old, Kelly was 2. They were playing in front of our house here.

A driver lost control and hit the children.

Terry's Mother: Terry was struck in the head and suffered a brain injury and crushed skull. Kelly had a skull fracture and a leg broken in 2 spots that required a full body cast, but Terry was injured the most severely.

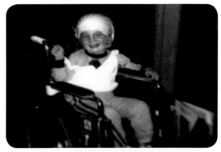

Terry's Father: He lost all his speech, he could not walk anymore and he lost use of his right hand. They told us the head injury was very bad and they did not know if he would live – they didn't think he would.

Yet somehow, his parents noted, the young boy's state of happiness didn't die.

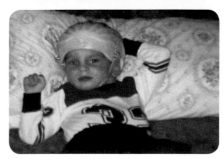

Terry's Mother: Everybody loves him. His doctor in Duluth had told us that Terry's a miracle, he's always called him that.

Today, Terry, the miracle, now in his late 20's, keeps happening.

Terry Knuti: Hello? Hello? Hello? I'm doing something important, I gotta go.

Terry lives alone with Austin his lab in a house he calls the hunting shack. But he's also no stranger to the sights and sounds of the great outdoors.

Terry: This is my first bear that I shot in...1993 I think, maybe 1991? I shot that bear in Canada and I shot this deer towards Giants Ridge.

Terry, the miracle, has become an unabridged outdoorsman.

Terry: I like the wilderness and I like the outdoors. I mostly ride 4-wheelers, snowmobile, and hunt. And I like to do stuff with animals...dogs and stuff.

Terry also goes hunting the hard way. With a bow and arrow.

Terry: I bite on this string, to pull it back, cause I can't use my other hand. I also can't close my one eye, and I have a hard time seeing.

Terry's Dad: We experimented with a few things, with rope and with tubing and serving string, and everything would seem to unravel. But he was able to draw it with the method he had. He was able to draw it with his teeth. And by 16 we even got him drawing a 48lb bow. In the summer we have an outdoor range and we shoot at these targets in the woods. Now it just goes to prove that you don't need a crossbow if you're handicapped, there's other ways to do that. And Terry's living proof of that.

As for Terry's future goals...well, they won't need a miracle.

Terry: Like I said, if I didn't get run over by a car and I was walking normal, I could probably get a girlfriend. Easily.

And then?????

Terry: I hope to be a famous D.J. or be a famous hunter like Ted Nugent (laughs).

Post Script: Terry has a part time job in town and operates his own D.J. business, playing music at booked parties. Terry also makes school visits to warn kids about alcohol and driving. The driver who hit him and his sister was suspected of DUI but was never charged.

Pet Steps to Heaven
LINDSTROM, MINNESOTA

Minnesota Bound viewers often ask — how do you find such great stories? The answer sometimes is, in strange ways. This story is a case in point. I was fishing in a bass tournament when a fella named John Laub paused to tell me about his dying dog. After the dog died, John said, his wife came up with an idea she called Pet Steps to Heaven. Would we be interested in such a story, John asked? I took the first step and said yes.

Patty Laub, Pet Steps to Heaven: This is glass – each piece is hand cut.

Ron's Narrative: This is a happy story about a sad ending.

Patty: You have to be real precise on these. This is a lab head I'm doing, this is for someone that had a black lab and they would like a nice remembrance of their best friend.

Patty Laub knows all about sad endings.

Patty: It's all about Zak, our German shorthair, which was the best dog we owned.

When Zak the family pet died at age 14, Patty Laub in her sadness came up with a happy ending.

Patty: I've done stained glass for 8 years and I've done stones before and I always said I was going to put my dog into a stepping stone for my garden.

And she came up with a name – Pet Steps to Heaven. But her idea needed one more thing. An answer on how to do it.

Patty: At first when people asked me at work, they kinda laughed oh sure, how are you going to get this dog into the stone? I didn't have any clue how to do this. Then after thinking about it for a while I thought well, what the heck and I dumped the ashes in and mixed it and away we went.

Comfort replaced Patty's sadness and now she's doing the same for other pet owners.

Patty: This is something nice for people that don't know what to do with their pets. A lot of people think of their pets as their children. I just think that when you have a pet, they're part of your family. And it's kinda a shame to just throw them away after they've given you years of pleasure.

She also had the skill needed in cutting glass, making molds and adding dignity.

Patty: There's nothing quite like this, but how many people like working with animal remains? It's not ishy, it's pretty nice. It's just like baking a cake (laughing).

And when the cake is done, it becomes a walk in the garden.

Patty: These are my displays. Out here we have Mister Buck – Mr. Buck is a lot of dog!

I get cats, a lot of dogs and I've been asked to do horses. With horses I do the bench, 3 or 4 stones, or a walkway.

Patty's idea is now a business in Lindstrom, Minnesota. Prices range from $140 to $170. But her Steps to Heaven are made of more than glass and cement.

Patty: The same amount of love and work goes into each one. My dream is to give this idea to everybody on what they can do.

Everybody just might need steps in that direction.

Post Script: When the original Raven died, her ashes – thanks to Patty – were mixed into a bench seat that was placed at the Two Rivers Wildlife Management Area in Southern, Minnesota. Raven helped raise money to acquire the Two Rivers land. Now visitors have a place to sit and contemplate the wild.

Purple Martin Man

If Purple Martins had red breasts, they would be everybody's favorite bird. Graceful flyers, insect eaters and family-oriented – Purple Martins have lots to admire. So do Purple Martin people. Everybody adores martins but nobody in the martin adoration society can match the martin magic of Don Wilkins.

Don Wilkins, The Purple Martin Man: How many pairs do I have here? I haven't done a count this year yet, but somewhere in the 80 to 90 range. I've got enough houses out there for just over 100 pairs.

Ron's Narrative: He's America's largest landlord to the Purple Martin. Meet Don Wilkins, a man devoted to one of nature's most graceful flyers.

Don: Oh, they're just a nice bird. They're such superb fliers, and they're just fun to watch. I can sit down there by the hour and just watch 'em gliding and they're particularly interesting when they're feeding young – It's just fun.

But Don, the Purple Martin Man, is more than a bird watcher.

Don: I've started doing some things in designing houses. The main thing is giving them protection from predators, particularly from owls, by making deep compartments or dividing compartments

If you get that nest box deep enough, then they will be out of the reach of the owls.

Long an icon on Minnesota lakes, the Purple Martin, you could say, is Minnesota's version of the Capistrano Swallow.

Don: I start looking for 'em real hard about the 15th of April. And then it'll be within a day or two. Then I'll go through and do a count. I'm a federally licensed bird bander so I've banded many martins, too.

Over the years, Wilkins has discovered something else about Purple Martins. They might be famous for eating mosquitoes, but is it true?

Don: Not for one second! That is absolute malarkey. I think it was spread by one of the manufacturers of Purple Martin houses. They'll say a martin will eat 2,000 mosquitoes a day. But here's why that can't be. The Purple Martins are flying during the daytime. How many mosquito bites do you get during the day? Now come 10 o'clock at night the mosquitoes might be trying to feed on you, but the martins are sleeping.

In truth, the martin landlord says, the birds prefer to eat dragonflies.

Don: I'm just going to go out and check that box and see what's nesting in it. Now you can't see it but there's two of 'em in there. Ok, here's a typical nest here, and you notice they bring in the green leaves? That's mostly the males that bring those in. The eggs are snow white – they'll lay anywhere from four to six, seven occasionally. I've seen eight, but I'm not sure it was by one bird.

I enjoy this and they get used to me. You'll notice they're coming in pretty close to me now, too. They're pretty confident in their flying ability. There isn't much that can catch 'em.

If you haven't guessed it by now, this is a Purple Martin love story that has lasted for more than 40 years.

Don: Purple Martins need help. They're not an endangered species, but they're scarce.

Purple Martins are now almost completely dependent on man-made nesting structures. This spring, as our eyes soar on their wings, here's something to ponder. It's up to us to keep our largest swallow returning to Minnesota.

The Bullhead Murders
WATERVILLE, MINNESOTA

We read every letter sent by viewers — and for good reason. One day a letter told us about the last surviving witness to one of Minnesota's worst murder cases involving state conservation officers in the town of Waterville. What's more, the murders were in the name of bullheads. With only one witness still alive to tell the story, we said we'd visit Minnesota's bullhead capitol faster than you can say whiskers.

Ron's Narrative: In Minnesota, the small country town of Waterville claims an undisputed title, fishing capital of the world for...bullheads. It's an unusual story, Waterville and bullheads. Today bullhead fishing in the lakes around Waterville is a summer tourist attraction. But one day years ago, catching bullheads became a motive for murder.

The year was 1940 and this building – its been remodeled now – belonged to a commercial fisherman from Waterville, Minnesota. He cleaned his fish here including bullheads, but on Friday afternoon July 12, 1940 this also became the bloodiest scene in the history of DNR law enforcement.

Linden Vail, Last Surviving Witness: I used to go out fishing by myself and my father would come down in the afternoon and he'd help me clean the bullheads.

But that afternoon, Linden Vail, age 13 at the time, was about to witness a triple murder.

Linden: We started to clean our fish and the game wardens were here.

Three Minnesota game wardens, Marcus Whipps, Melvin Holt and Dudley Brady had come to see a commercial fisherman by the name of Bryant Baumgartner.

Linden: When we came they were kind of talking back and forth and my father could kind of see what was going on, and he said to Bryant we'll leave and come back later and Bryant said they won't bother you people just keep cleaning your fish.

Bryant Baumgartner was suspected of illegally catching and selling bullheads. The wardens asked to see his commercial fishing license.

Linden: And he said I will go get it and to this day – it's just like a Hollywood movie because he walked towards the house back here and those 3 men walked out of the fish market and went in a circle. Whipps went to the right and Holt stood right in front of me and Brady was off to my left.

When Bryant came out of the house he was holding this shotgun and without saying a word he aimed at the game wardens and opened fire.

And that was it. It was boom, boom, boom.

Boom – Warden Marcus Whipps, 45, fell face down in a flower garden. Boom – Hit in the chest, Officer Melvin Holt, 55, dropped in his tracks.

Boom – Officer Dudley Brady turned to run but was hit by the third shot.

Ron Schara: So when the shooting happened what did you see?

Linden: Whipps fell over there in the flower bed and about this far Holt fell here in front of me. I was this close to him cause I felt the pellets flying around and then Brady was over right in this area here and fell there.

MARCUS EMERSON WHIPPS

Marcus Whipps, 45, was born on 3 February 1895 in Kasota and grew up there. He enlisted in the Navy in World War I. He was married to Caroline Beiser in 1923 and worked in the stone quarries at Kasota for some time after their marriage. He then worked as a policeman for the town of Kasota. He had been a Game Warden for about three years at the time he was killed.

Funeral services for Game Warden Marcus Whipps were held from the Presbyterian Church at Kasota on Monday, 15 July 1940. Burial was in Greenwood Woodlawn Cemetery south of LeCenter. He was survived by his wife, Caroline, two daughters, a son, his mother, two sisters and a brother. Six Game Wardens served as pall bearers. They were G. F. Huber of

A. MELVIN HOLT

Game Warden A. Melvin Holt, 55, was born at Preston, Minnesota, and spent his early years at LeRoy. In 1921 he moved to Bagley and started working for the Forest Service. On 1 March 1926 he was appointed as a salaried Game Warden for the Department of Game and Fish. He worked in that capacity (with a few intermittent lay-offs because of funding shortages) in Bagley until 1 March of 1940, when he transferred to Worthington. He had completed thirteen and one-quarter years of service as a Game Warden when he was murdered.

Game Warden A. Melvin Holt was survived by his wife, a son (Roland), a daughter in Seattle (Dorothy), two parents, three sisters and a brother. His funeral was held in Lake City on Tuesday, 16 July 1940, with many Game Wardens in attendance. Also attending were E. R. Stark,

Without saying a word, the enraged bullhead fisherman reloaded his Remington Model 11 and turned the gun on himself.

Linden: There was a picket fence over here and he leaned the gun up against the fence and it wasn't but a matter of seconds and that was it.

Ron: And 4 people were dead.

Linden: Four people had died. That's when my dad said we were going and I could hear Baumgartner moaning and groaning when I went by him but I never looked at him.

In big headlines and graphic pictures, Waterville and its bullheads made the news.

Town Resident: It was a warm day the 12th of July 1940 when nobody had air conditioners and the houses got hot – nobody had fans back then even. And I remember dogs howling all over town that night I don't know if the dogs sensed it – I can still remember that part, I couldn't sleep all night.

Today the sleepless nights are gone. And the old fish market is now somebody's remodeled home. As for the town's historic murders, well, only a dwindling few remember.

Town Resident: I think of it every once in awhile.

For years the murder weapon was displayed at a corner bar. As for the suspected bullhead killer, well, he never left town either. He's buried in the city cemetery.

Post Script: A year after the Waterville wardens were killed in the line of duty, the State of Minnesota issued uniforms and sidearms to its enforcement agents, now known as conservation officers. Each surviving family of the killed wardens received a $7,500 death benefit, although it arrived a year late.

Catching bullheads became a
motive for murder.

The Greatest Fishing Lure Story Ever Told

In the world today, the **most popular** fishing lure is known as the Rapala. It is made in Finland. But few people know the Finnish lure also has a **close connection to Minnesota.** In fact, the **lure's fame** can be traced back to two Minnesota businessmen, Ron Weber and Ray Ostrom. Ron and Ray knew a **good lure when they saw one** – they also knew how to sell it. The result was the greatest fishing lure story ever told.

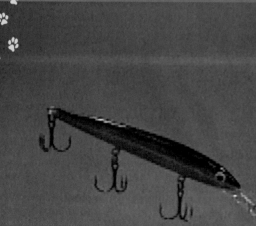

Ron's Narrative: A half century ago, a poor fisherman sat at his workbench in far away Finland, carving fishing lures from the inner bark of pine trees. His story begins like a fairy tale. Because as a boy the wood carver never knew his real name. His adopted parents simply gave him a name – Lauri Rapala.

Jarmo Rapala, Grandson: Lauri loved fishing. Oh yeah, he loved fishing to the end. In the beginning he had to feed his family by catching fish. It was work. But the passion was there all the time.

Lauri Rapala's passion changed history. As he carved his lure and carved it again, he unknowingly created what would become the greatest selling fishing lure of all time.

Little did he know that someday millions of Rapala lures – $100 million dollars worth – would land in tackle boxes every year.

Jarmo: I think it would be very difficult for him to understand the success. On the other hand he would be very pleased to see the success for his family and the people of his hometown.

Today Lauri Rapala is respected as a national hero in Finland. However, it was an honor he never knew. Lauri Rapala died in 1974 at the age of 68.

Lars Ollberg, Rapala Executive: The good thing is, the lure's quality hasn't changed because we understand the history, we appreciate the history and we know where we're coming from.

In a Rapala factory in Vaaksy, Finland, some 300 families work there. The lure making begins with wood – with wood here, wood there and imported from Ecuador.

Jari Kokkonen, Rapala Executive: They are farming those trees on a farm so we are not cutting the rain forest.

What Lauri Rapala once did with his hands, machines carve now. Twenty-four hours a day – strips of wood take shape as lure bodies to the dictates of computerized designs.

Jari: These are very fast and they are very precise.

The making of a Rapala becomes a lesson in ingenuity. Machines grinding, gauges jumping and things tumbling. Things like lure lips. But for some lure making tasks, human hands still must do the work.

Jari: You can see how they put the foil on the lure; it's handwork. It cannot be done with the machines. You have to be very skillful and precise so the result is as good as they are.

Each Rapala lure design has different needs. So many styles, so many colors. But every Rapala is only as good as it swims on the end of the line. Annie the lure tester, has the final say.

Annie, The Lure Tester: This lure is ready to catch fish.

Ron Schara: Guaranteed?

Annie: There is a Rapala guarantee, if you don't catch fish it's your own fault.

Lauri Rapala's fame as a lure carver may have had humble beginnings, but in 1962 he had a major league boost from blond bombshell, Marilyn Monroe. By chance, Marilyn was on the cover of Life Magazine when the editors ran a story about Lauri Rapala entitled the lure fish can't resist.

A pair of Minnesota businessmen/anglers, Ron Weber and his partner Ray Ostrom, were marketing Rapalas in the U.S. and Canada.

Ron Weber: There was good news and bad news. People sent us envelopes of money to buy Rapalas. The bad news was we didn't have many. To meet the demand, Weber's company, Normark, helped Lauri Rapala and sons build larger plants to increase production. By 1975, 25 million Rapala lures had been sold.

The rest, as they say, is history.

As a poor fisherman trying to feed his family, Lauri Rapala carved lures and tested them in a place called Paijanne Lake. On an island on Paijanne, there's a log cabin where Lauri Rapala would stay for the night. Today, the crude dwelling is akin to an angling shrine.

According to the legend about a half-century ago Lauri Rapala used to stop here after a hard day of fishing. Joined by a fishing friend, they'd tell stories, carve some lures and give a toast of vodka to the day's fishing success.

Visitors to this cabin still do the same. Here's a toast to you, Lauri Rapala (Ron drinks a shot of vodka).

He loved fishing...
In the beginning he had to
feed his family by catching fish.
It was work.

But the passion was there
all the time.

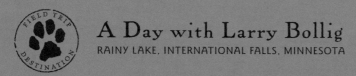

A Day with Larry Bollig
RAINY LAKE, INTERNATIONAL FALLS, MINNESOTA

I first met Larry Bollig at a Mille Lacs fishing tournament. He was an unknown with a deep, hoarse voice and a face made for radio. You wouldn't want to meet Larry in a dark alley. I quickly learned that behind that tough exterior, Larry Bollig was a gentle man with an intense love of fishing. That discovery would lead to years of friendship and many days of fishing companionship. As time went on, however, I saw less of Larry. We were both busy. Besides, Larry had become a local celebrity doing "Bear Facts and Fish Tales" on KSTP Radio with Rapala Fishing Pro, Mark Fisher.

One day we made a promise to each other to fish together again. We picked a date in early September. And, as promised, we met on Rainy Lake in International Falls, Minnesota. It was high noon and the start of a memorable day with The Bear.

Ron Schara: There's some - I got something! Nice smallmouth, oh and it's a big one. Yeah look at it. Ooh, that's a big fish.

Larry Bollig: That's a big one, yeah.

Ron: That is one big fish.

Ron's Narrative: While this Rainy Lake smallmouth bass swims below the boat, we should pause to meet the fella in the fancy fishing pants.

Larry: These pants drive me crazy.

His name is Larry Bollig. Fishing pants aside, he's not crazy unless the definition applies to catching fish.

Larry: When you really get onto the fish in the fall and you catch one after the other and you say oh it's only a 3 pounder – and you want to hurry up and reel it in.

Oh Ron, that's a good fish. Ohh, is that a beauty. This is really a big fish.

That's the way to start the day. That's a five pound smallmouth bass.

So begins our crazy angling adventure with Larry, "The Bear" Bollig. Crazy about fishing. Crazy about Rainy Lake. And he talks to every fish he releases.

Larry: Bye, bye honey.

Almost everything about Larry Bollig is rather unusual. Raised in the small town of Pierz, Minnesota, he's a blue collar worker who turned tournament angler and evolved into a radio celebrity.

Ron: Were you nervous about starting a radio show?

Larry: Well, I'm a ham. But I've done a lot of seminars in my life, so speaking about fishing is not hard for me to do. And that's all I'm doing. We try to have fun and make people laugh. I say don't take yourself too seriously. It's fun.

For Larry, however, fishing is a serious subject. And he harbors strong opinions about his angling passion.

Larry: One of the biggest problems I have with the DNR is that they don't have enough law enforcement conservation officers.

And fish biologists? Fisheries and biologists are good in the DNR as long as they believe in fishing even if they don't fish themselves.

And lead sinker bans? Can I use the word asinine on the show? We have more loons today than we had 30 years ago, no question about that. I think it's a feel-good issue. If I knew the loon was gonna disappear because of lead sinkers, I would throw mine away. But you can't tell me what I can't see. I can see the loon population is healthy. It's healthy as heck. To ban sinkers is not good for the economy right now and it would serve no worthwhile cause. I'm against it.

Ron: And if you were the king, Larry?

Larry: I like that question. I'd have a crown right now and you'd be bowing.

In Larry Bollig's kingdom every weekend from May to October is spent on scenic Rainy Lake, a maze of islands and fishing water shared between Minnesota and Ontario. And Larry knows just about every rock.

Larry: I decided to rent a house up here, because I was coming up 18 - 20 weekends a year. I come up in the wintertime and ice fish too.

Oops, here's a fish on. I don't think this can be a bass. I got a feeling this is a northern pike.

Ron: You need some help?

Larry: Yeah, dive in and get him. Oh man, come here fish. That's a nice pike – a 10 to 12 pounder. That is a beautiful fish. That fish will be a 25 pounder someday because I'm releasing it.

You know what I like about Rainy? Rainy Lake is one of the few lakes that you can't learn in a lifetime.

There we go. You got one?

Ron: Yup. A little better one, but he still looks small compared to the one you got.

As our fish catches began to mount, we began to believe the unlikely. This was starting to be one heck of a fishing trip.

Larry: Ooh look at the size of that one. I got 'em. Ooh it's another big one. I think he's gonna get off. That's ok. If you wanna leave me that's ok. Easy there big fella. Yes, that's a nice fish. Goodbye.

Ron: Do you always say goodbye to your fish?

Larry: Yeah, because you know they might come back. They're not real bright.

Ron: There's one. Oh he's a nice one. They have a lot of heart.

Larry: Normally in the fall up here you can't really have a bad day.

The bass and walleyes of Rainy Lake must have been listening.

Larry: Oh man that thing has got power this one is gonna be a while – oh is she plump. Oh my golly. That's a five pounder – might even be six.

The next catch? We had two at a time.

Larry: Oh look, there are 2 of 'em. Look at it, look at it. They're both hooked. You got 'em both! Two at a time! Two at a time! Isn't that something?

And then our fishing luck got even better.

Larry: Here fishy, fishy, fishy.

Ron: There's a good fish. Ooh it's a good fish – I think it's a big walleye.

Larry: Oh, it is a big walleye!

Ron: That is a big walleye – it's huge. This could be the biggest walleye I've ever caught in my life.

Larry: Is that a fatty atty or what? That's an 8 to 9 pound walleye easy. Hey – it's a 10 pounder Schara! Alright!! This doesn't happen. We got about a 14 pound northern, two bass over 5 pounds, a 10 pound walleye and 3 to 4 smaller walleyes.

So you can see, we went fishing with The Bear because there's seldom a dull moment.

Larry: This is wonderful!

Hard to believe, but wonderful, for sure.

Field Trip Location

Rainy Lake is one of the few lakes that you can't learn in a lifetime.

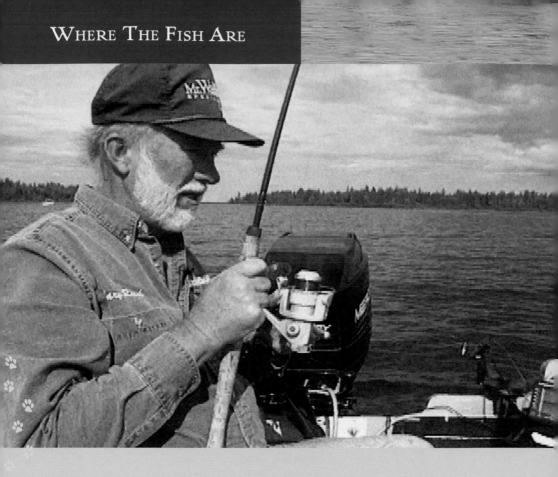

A Day with Gary Roach
CANADA'S CAMP KINISOO AT LAC LA RONGE, SASKATCHEWAN

I first met Gary Roach more than 35 years ago. We were fishing together on a Wisconsin lake. Gary was a hard working Minnesota fishing guide who had come to Wisconsin to help his buddies, Al and Ron Lindner, promote the Lindy Rig. I had an immediate liking for Gary. He was easy going, and he liked music and cocktails when the fishing day was over. Our day together launched a lifetime friendship, although we don't brag much about our first fishing trip. We got skunked. Now Gary Roach is one of America's most famous anglers. Go figure.

Ron's Narrative: If you met him just standing on a boat dock, you might not realize this bearded man with a friendly face is also the Babe Ruth of walleye fishing in America. Fact is, he's known as Mr. Walleye.

It's a registered trademark that launched Gary Roach into the big leagues of professional fishing.

To fans of walleye tournaments, Gary Roach is a celebrity, a fishing star who's recognized in restaurants, and whose name adorns all kinds of fishing gear as if Babe Ruth himself was signing fishing rods.

When he's not competing in walleye tournaments, Roach spends time at his Minnesota lake cabin often cleaning fish and later frying up fillets in batter from a box that has his name.

Ron Schara: Any cooking secrets?

Gary Roach: Cleaning the fish and eating them as soon as you catch 'em. I tell you what – there's nothing better than the fresh ones.

Yet, it's not the kitchen where Mr. Walleye feels most at home. When he goes fishing it's like watching a master artist at work.

Gary: Are we ready to go? I'll get my guide sunglasses on. All I see through these glasses are 8 pound walleyes.

It's a trip to Canada's Camp Kinisoo at Lac La Ronge, Saskatchewan.

Gary: Yah, I've been up since five. Got my rod in the boat and had three or four cups of coffee.

He might have been fishing yesterday but Gary Roach always looks forward to fishing today.

Gary: I always listen to my walleye. He talks to me all the time and tells me what he wants.

Gary Roach is happiest when the walleye is on his end of the line. And when the master gets hot, no walleye is uncatchable. And so it goes. Walleye after walleye,

Ron: There's one fish for me. That's the fish of the day, huh?

But it's always a bigger walleye for the master.

Gary: Another nice fish, a fighter. Oh a dandy. Mine is always bigger than yours.

One day at Knee Lake in Manitoba, my walleye fishing luck was getting warm...

Gary: That Ron Schara is my idol.

Ron: I'm the new Mr. Walleye

Gary: Catch too many and your apt to lose your hat. Hey, I've just caught a big one too, Mr. Schara. It means I'm only one behind you.

And that's the way it is in a fishing boat with Gary Roach. Fish and fun. I should know. Over the years we've caught a ton of walleyes together. And always Gary has caught the most.

Ron: Hey Gary, remember the first time we went fishing? You tell 'em what we caught.

Gary: Nothing.

For Gary Roach, no doubt, it was the last time he caught nothing.

Gary Roach is a celebrity,
a fishing star who's
recognized in
restaurants, and whose name
adorns all kinds of fishing gear as if
Babe Ruth himself was
signing fishing rods.

A Fairly Reliable Fishing Guide
RAINY LAKE, MINNESOTA

He's a Rainy Lake fishing guide who goes by the name of Woody. You really don't meet Woody. Woody meets you. He's a marketing genius who doesn't know it. Through the years, Minnesota Bound has traveled far and wide with Woody. We sometimes catch fish but we always have fun. We also were lucky. Woody says he's such a talented guide that 90 percent of his customers return safely to the dock.

Ron's Narrative: When Woody is your fishing guide, there's never a dull moment on the end of the line or in the boat. Meet Barry Joseph Woods. More famously known as Woody. He is president and CEO of Woody's Fairly Reliable Guide Service. A job he's held since age 13.

And all of it on vast Rainy Lake, which straddles the border between northern Minnesota and Ontario, Canada.

Woody: It's wilderness water where most of the lake homes belong to the beaver. And the noisiest neighbors are loons. What's special and unique is we have a diverse fishery, smallmouth, largemouth, crappies, muskies, sturgeon, walleye, sauger and whitefish.

Oh, a big fish just jumped out there. Did you see that Ron?

A fishing adventure with Woody is often just that. More adventure than fishing.

Woody: I really love guiding. It's like taking a trip everyday without leaving the farm. It's not a lifestyle that lends itself to making money. But you're on vacation all the time, too.

Woody's first rule of business is to have fun fishing or better yet, make it fun.

Woody: At my pub, you're welcome to bring your Rapala and your Visa card. That's because I don't mind a hook in the ass but Woody won't take American Express. That's my act. Maybe I belong in Hollywood (laughs).

Rainy Lake is famed for walleyes but the sleeper fish of this wilderness lake is its abundant smallmouth bass.

Woody: I like bass but I'm not going to kiss it.

Woody knows smallmouth don't mind sucking up a night crawler.

Woody: Look at that one, a dandy. That's a big bass. That could be a world record.

Yah, you betcha, Woody.

Woody: I hooked 'em right in the lip. It's gold baby, not bronze, it's gold. We're gonna let that baby go back and grow up a little more.

A Rainy Lake sunset turns Woody into a philosopher.

Woody: This place courses through my veins. It's just the most gorgeous lake in the world. Days like this you don't want to end.

A day with Woody is the same.

It's wilderness water where most of the lake homes belong to the beaver. And the noisiest neighbors are loons.

Field Trip Location

Meet the Babe

It's no secret Minnesotans have a passion for hunting, fishing, camping or just being out in nature. It may explain why Minnesota is also home to so many national outdoor television celebrities. In fact, I think there may be **more Minnesota - based shows** on television than any other state.

One of the pioneers in fishing shows is a fella named Babe Winkelman. **When I first met Babe**, he was in the family's construction business in St. Cloud. He also was an avid fisherman who yearned to switch careers. One day he asked my advice about getting into the fishing business. I told him to work on his writing and speaking. I also had a hand in one of **his first big breaks** — appearing on a television commercial for a mosquito repellant.

Babe was an instant hit and the rest is history.

Ron's Narrative: There's a Babe in every sport, it seems. Meet the Babe of fishing. Babe Winkelman.

Babe Winkleman: Not everything that glitters is gold. Many think it's cool to fish for a living. I tell folks you fish all day and well, I finally got sick of telling people the truth because they wouldn't believe me anyway, so I said man you can't imagine how cool it is, a buddy will come over and we'll take off for a couple of days, come home and the money comes out of the mail box. I might as well tell them that, because they won't believe how hard a person has to work or what you have to do.

For more than two decades, Donald Edward Winkelman, a former construction worker from St. Cloud, Minnesota has been the Babe of good fishing television shows on cable networks nationwide.

Ron Schara: So this is where it all happens.

Babe: All that scenery comes in electronically, don't ask me how they do it, but your always in a pretty spot.

And it all began when Babe, a regular Minnesota fisherman did a television commercial for a mosquito repellent. Somebody suggested Babe ought to have his own fishing show.

Babe: Dad told me, your not the smartest on the street, but I will tell you this, if you use our God given common sense you learn you can beat 99 percent of the folks because they are lazy. Our success is attributed to a great work ethic from the farm.

Today on Babe's farm the crop is a bumper of fishing and hunting shows, a stable of sponsors and a schedule that sends him on the road upwards of 250 days a year.

Babe: But this is not a job Ron, it's not a business, it's my life. Every cell of my body, every ounce of energy, every moment of thought process I have, it's involved with my life. I set my life up so that I could truly do what I want to do.

Most importantly to me is that we're able to capture the most important element of the outdoors and that is family spending time outdoors. The outdoors, my gosh you don't have to teach your kid about the creator if he spends enough time outdoors, it soaks in and that's what the outdoors is all about.

And when he's not fishing or hunting or in the office, the Babe retreats to an outdoorsy home full of hunting and fishing mementos.

And an old dream. Babe the guitar picker.

Babe: (Singing) But those trains keep a rolling down that San Antone.

People ask me when are you gonna retire Babe? When I die! What are you gonna do sit back and rock? I can't ever sit still.

In Babe's world, rocking the boat is good.

All About Sturgeon
RAINY RIVER, MINNESOTA

We seldom think about the poor fish. With walleyes, muskie, bass and **other glamorous critters** to catch in Minnesota, who cares for the ugly sturgeon. Well, you might be surprised to learn the sturgeon is one of Minnesota's rarest fish, but it's making a comeback in the Rainy River. **Finally, somebody cares about the ugly sturgeon.** It was a love story we just had to tell.

Ron's Narrative: Rivers were just rivers before we started dividing up the earth. Now this river, the Rainy River represents a flowing international border line between the U.S. and Canada. While deer live on both sides and pelicans cross the international border with a wing flap, there is more intrigue flowing between the river's banks.

Angler: Anything eating your bait?

In the depths of the Rainy River lives one of North America's strangest fish. And one of its rarest. It's called the Lake Sturgeon.

Mike Hanson, DNR Fish Biologist: A sturgeon is a fish that feeds off the bottom. They've been in this river for literally thousands of years. Interestingly, it's a prehistoric boneless survivor from the days of dinosaurs.

Most anglers don't even realize the fish exists as it's seldom seen. But the Rainy River population of sturgeon once was nearly decimated by excessive commercial netting. Today, the sturgeon numbers are coming back but it is a slow recovery. And sport anglers face severe restrictions for catching and keeping a sturgeon.

DNR Biologist: The restrictions haven't changed anglers' enthusiasm. They can still come out here to catch those fish and it's getting more popular all the time.

Oh yes, this prehistoric fish has one more enticing characteristic. It's the largest freshwater game fish in Minnesota and it's capable of reaching weights of 100 pounds or more. To catch one, just plunk to the river bottom a gob of something smelly, such as nightcrawlers.

DNR Biologist: Their reproductive capabilities are low. Females don't mature until they are about 26 years old. Then they spawn once every 4 to 9 years and the males are 19 when they first spawn. Then they spawn every other year. It just takes a long time for them to reach their reproductive capabilities.

The best news for the Lake Sturgeon is anglers are learning to admire its spunk and they are working to increase sturgeon numbers.

DNR Biologist: The best part is seeing how excited they get. They get a smile on their face that death wouldn't wash off!

A smile that won't wash off is just another reason to make sure this international river monster is around for another million years.

Field Trip Location

It's the largest freshwater game fish in Minnesota and it's capable of reaching weights of 100 pounds or more.

Bluegill Bro
SECRET BLUEGILL HOTSPOT

One of the joys of being a story teller is meeting a good story. I've seen my share of spectacular sunsets, gorgeous mountain tops, giant waterfalls and the like. I've been humbled by the majestic flights of Sandhill cranes, herds of migrating elk and a sky so full of snow geese it seemed they could barely fly. But nothing tops meeting a new and interesting character, somebody who has an absolute passion for what they do, what they believe in. Such is the story of a young fisherman who is much wiser than his age. He loves big bluegills. And that's good. Big bluegills are one of Minnesota's rarest catches.

On this day, we met Bluegill Bro' who promised to show us what a big bluegill looked like. We also promised to keep secret his lake. Can these bluegill giants be saved from extinction? They can, if Bluegill Bro' has his way.

Ron Schara: Ok what's the first step bro?

Bluegill Bro: We're gonna get on a nice weed edge. It's the middle of summer and the bluegills are moving to the weed line.

Ron's Narrative: He calls himself Bro. Bro, the bluegill specialist. No cabins here.

Bluegill Bro: This is how they all were – isn't that something – a throwback in time.

And it's a throwback time for bluegills. Yes, Bro is a catch and release hunter of giant bluegills.

Bluegill Bro: I like to see them thrown back because that's what keeps the lake alive and the bigger ones in the lake – they protect the nest and keep the little ones from spawning.

Bro was born Brian Brosdahl. A decade ago Bro headed north from Minneapolis, Minnesota, launched a fish guiding service and never returned.

Bluegill Bro: It's not a real high – money way to make a living, but if you stay busy you can live comfortable. You do it because you love it.

Although he typically guides for walleyes and such. His passion is for catching bluegills, especially big gills.

Bluegill Bro: I've always loved catching bluegills, but I really started pursuing them as they started disappearing. It was getting harder and harder to find them. Bluegill spots are coveted and very secretive – and it was the lure of catching something that's rare.

So rare are big bluegills – those weighing 1 pound or more – that Bro has launched his own campaign to protect them.

Bluegill Bro: If the fish really start hitting strong, I got circle hooks so they won't get gut hooked. And if we want to release the bigger fish, the hooks won't damage them. They will get hooked in the lip every time. Let me get the leeches out.

Ron: I was wondering what the secret bait would be.

Bluegill Bro: It's still leeches but crawlers are starting to come into play. Here's one of those baby leeches...and you hook it thru the sucker.

Ron: Come on gills.

Bluegill Bro: Way to go Ron – a bluegill…that's just a start.

Ron: At least it's the right kind. Is that a male or female?

Bluegill Bro: That's a female, the males usually have a little red or pink in them.

Ron: Oh there we go, wow there's a bluegill – that's a big one. That's not a pound though is it?

Bluegill Bro: No, it's not a pound. This is about a 10 ouncer, it's some people's pound (laugh). What a beautiful fish, we'll let that one go.

They fight pound for...ounce for ounce I should say. They fight better than just about any gamefish. They really give it a good battle. Plus they spin – what other fish spins in a tight circle like that. And when they bite they really bite.

Ron: It's a good one I think. I haven't got as many big bluegills as you have. Oh yeah, he's really fighting. A big old pumpkin seed (fish comes into the boat). Oh look at that (laughing) isn't that a pie plate as they say. It's a beauty – aren't they gorgeous – that fluorescent blue.

Bluegill Bro: The last decade or the whole time I've been guiding I've appreciated catching these big things, and I stopped keeping them a while back. It just seemed like when people would go through, they'd catch 'em out of a lake. And it didn't take much to catch 'em out. I've seen it over and over. Now we have very few lakes that have big bluegills.

There's four quarters to fishing: there's the search, the actual fishing, the catching and the eating. Well, I like the first three quarters. And I do like the fourth quarter. I will eat gills, but they have to be smaller and there's no reason to kill a big gill.

We really should get some trophy – class lakes set aside, designated trophy – class lakes. And the bluegills will thrive, because they're in the lake, and they could be recycled. Then you know you would have a place to go to catch real big bluegills.

In Bro's world, large bluegills deserve to be caught more than once.

His passion is for catching bluegills, especially big gills.

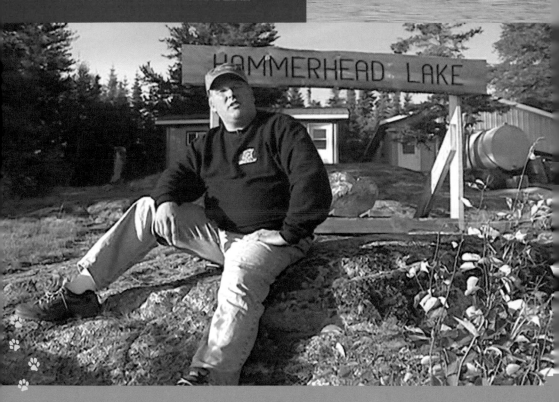

Brotherly Love
HAMMERHEAD LAKE, ONTARIO

I was raised in a family of anglers, starting with grandparents, aunts, uncles, father, and mother. Fishing fever eventually spread to my brothers and sisters. Since I'm the oldest, it struck me first. Since I was the first to fish, my younger siblings have spent the rest of their lives trying to out fish me. It's good old fashioned sibling rivalry, I suppose. What's more, it never goes away. My brothers and I took a Canada fishing trip one time and, bingo, there it was again...ancient rivalries.

Ron Schara: You ready to catch some walleyes boys?

Notice I'm doing all the carrying (laughing).

Ron's Narrative: Bush Pilot Eddie Showalter has never had a load of fishermen quite like this one.

A short flight later, to Eddie's Outpost Camp on Ontario's Hammerhead Lake, the boys deplane.

Eddie Showalter: Watch your step gang.

Gang is a good word. This is the Schara gang, three brothers and one wannabe. Starting with the oldest, there's me, Ron, then brother Robert, then brother Rick. And this is Steve Herth. He's a good friend, and he wishes he was a brother. Well, sort of.

We've gathered at Eddie's Hammerhead Outpost Camp to scratch an intense family itch. Fishing, fishing, fishing.

Ron: You watch, pretty soon these two brothers are going to yell fish on...it's unspoken, but there's a lot of competition right now...who ever gets a fish first will have bragging rights. That's a lot of pressure when you're fishing with your brothers.

Rick Schara: You got the magic spot?

Ron: Yeah, we'll go way up through here. Time to find a walleye...I ended up with the map (laughing).

Robert Schara: I lost him. I had him on and lost him.

You don't know pressure until you fish with the Schara brothers.

Ron: There we go! Oh yeah, that's what we're after, golden walleye, and I'm the first brother to get one, that's what makes it better. I'm gonna keep this one just to prove it.

Ricky! (Rick holds up fish) Good job!

Rick: You got one?

Ron: What did we bring those two other guys along for? Oh yeah, shore lunch!

Rick: It takes a Schara to show 'em how to fish. Ron's got one.

Every dog has his day.

Of course, its even sweeter when the dog happens to be a brother.

You see, the Schara's have a family secret. We all have the same middle name. Tease.

Steve Herth: The way I got started with this crew is Rick was my college roommate at Iowa State...that's where I got my start with the Scharas. They call me the Schara wannabe, but I don't think they give me any harder time than they give each other, so I can't complain. In fact, I probably get less than they give each other.

Robert: It's the camaraderie. And we always tease each other – we grew up always being teased by our uncles and we tease each other about fishing and it's just something we've always done. And we laugh about it and we do some stupid stuff, but it's always a lot of fun.

Rick: I think Schara fishing goes back to our father and mother who took us on the Mississippi. Fishing taught us a lot about patience and I also think they gave us some of our humor too.

Ron: I like fishing with my brothers, it's always interesting because we go back so long. With family all of the old stories get retold, and the laughs are still there, so you relive a lot and that makes it fun.

Robert: We always razz each other about who's a better fisherman and we always get on each other about that.

But Robert, isn't your older brother the best walleye fisherman?

Robert: I don't think I'll go there...I would tell you after the camera is off.

Ask the question: Who's the best fisherman? I think you'll get 3 answers.

Robert: Who's the best fisherman? Hey you're looking at him (laughs).

So – that's the way it goes when the Schara brothers gather to go fishing.

We fish a bunch.

Robert: There we go! There's what we came for!

Rick: There Steve got one...nice walleye.

And we laugh a lot.

Rick: I think it's a walleye... a little fella (laughs).

Ron: Rick's got a little one (laughs).

Both our parents are gone now, but the thing that they planted with us – fishing as a family – we still do and it's nice to know that the tradition that my parents started still goes on.

'There's a lot of **competition** right now...who ever gets a fish first will have **bragging** rights.

Comeback of Lake Michigan
STURGEON BAY, WISCONSIN

I'll never forget the first time I saw Lake Michigan. I was about 12 and had never seen water with no distant shore. I had never seen a ship leave port and slowly sink into the water until only a smoke stack remained. I also vividly remember my fishing luck that day. It was awful. Here was this huge lake with hardly any fish. Just a few perch. And they were embarrassingly small.

Now fast forward to the 1970's when a new cry could be heard over Lake Michigan — Fish on. Coho and Chinook salmon had been introduced to the lake and the stocking was a huge success. Anglers were giddy with fish catching delight. Sadly, the salmon boom was short — lived because of fish disease problems. Today, those problems are being solved. So we returned to Sturgeon Bay, Wisconsin on Lake Michigan to see if anglers were once again shouting, Fish on.

Guide: Here you go Ron, you got a good fish here. It's a nice one. Let him pull and tire him out and reel when you can.

Ron Schara: Got a little weight there.

Guide: It's a really nice fish – that's a dandy, yeah real nice. Probably an 8 - 9 pound fish. It's a King salmon.

Ron's Narrative: Yes, it's a King salmon but not just any salmon. A salmon swimming here in Lake Michigan, swims in one of the greatest fishing stories of our time.

Ron: That is a dandy, it is a dandy.

Salmon Biologist: If you remember back to the late sixties the lake had been overrun by alewives. Because the predators had all been eliminated by sea lampreys, so it was a system that was way out of production, way out of whack.

To the surprise of everyone, the Pacific salmon, which normally are at home in the ocean, thrived in their new freshwater environment.

Biologist: It grew rather slowly at first. They were putting in tens of thousands of salmon, and those numbers built up to hundreds of thousands and eventually to millions. It became a phenomenal fishery. Almost too good.

For Captain Jack Tong and Captain John Steiben, it's the start of another day on their version of paradise – a charter boat named Katiebird, chugging to salmon rich waters via Wisconsin's Sturgeon Bay Canal.

Captain Steiben: Mighty Michigan for me is the big King. There's nowhere in the Midwest where you'll see the big Kings in these numbers. That's what we're looking for. That's the fish we're here for.

Captain Steiben: You get a good burn in your arm fighting the kings. It gets hectic, you know. You can get 5 to 6 fish on at a time. They fight good and they're good to eat.

Fish on!!! Here you go Ron. Nope he's gone. How'd that salmon get off?

Finding the right lure pattern is done by trial and error.

Captain Steiben: There are different colors. One gives off a glow, and another gives off a flash. There's not a whole lot to it. That's the reason we run so many rods. Typically we start seeing the Kings here about mid – June. They're here until they make their runs to spawn in late September and early October.

It is a September morning on Lake Michigan and onboard the Katiebird, the hunt for salmon is only getting better.

Captain Steiben: This is a magical place for big salmon, no other place like it in the Midwest.

But the salmon magic begins in late autumn at, in this case, a place known as Strawberry Creek. It's where the salmon come to spawn and die.

Salmon Biologist: We've been stocking Chinook salmon in Lake Michigan since 1979. There is no natural reproduction of them, so if we want to continue to have Chinook salmon in Lake Michigan then we have to collect eggs each fall to stock out the next spring.

Each spring we bring about 200,000 of the Chinook salmon fingerlings here to Strawberry Creek and we imprint them so they think this is where they were hatched.

Then they go out to the lake and they spend anywhere from two to four summers out on the lake. When they mature they are looking for a place to spawn and they remember this place. So they swim right back up Strawberry Creek and jump right up in the pond for us. We collect the eggs, harvest the adults and start the process all over again.

If Wisconsin's fisheries didn't collect the eggs and restock Lake Michigan, the salmon boom would be a quick bust.

Salmon Biologist: About 15 million trout and salmon a year are stocked in Lake Michigan collectively by the four states and the federal government. This includes Chinook salmon, Coho salmon, Lake trout, Brown trout, Steelhead or Rainbow trout and Brook trout.

Three to four years later, the Chinook that began as an egg is now an eating machine in Lake Michigan with a tireless fighting heart.

Ron: When you have a King on the end of the line, you just hang on. That's all you can do. Hey, I think I'm running out of line.

Captain Steiben: We're gonna back up and see if we can get him under control. Get ready to reel.

A Chinook with broad shoulders had us in a stand – off.

Ron: I'm not tired, but we're backing on him and he's keeping the line tight.

What seemed like a month later, the big Chinook was in reach of the net.

Ron: Ohh he's huge – he is huge. Look at the size of that guy. Ohh, is he a 4 year old? Yikes. What's he gonna weigh, John.

Captain Steiben: He's a 4 year old salmon in the 30 pound class.

Ron: Now that's a fish, he's as tired as I am.

And the greatest fishing story in America adds another chapter.

There's nowhere in the Midwest where you'll see the **big kings** in these numbers.

Fishy Entrepreneurs
SCANDIA, MINNESOTA

We're always looking for stories that relate to fishing, hunting, nature and the like. So my **ears perked the day I heard** about a Koi raising farm in Minnesota. It was a good story, yes. But, then, it got better as we learned the fish farm was operated by **two teenage brothers** whom we later tagged the Koi Boys.

Father: This used to be a horse barn and a motorcycle shop. We gutted this building and built all this.

Mike: Yeah, we're the only ones like this in the state.

Ron's Narrative: Meet the Swanson brothers. Mike and Devin, who live on a small acreage near Scandia, Minnesota.

Devin: It looks really complicated but it's really not.

Easy to say when you're the head honchos of a fishy business.

Mike: This tank, those black discs on the bottom – those are bottom drains and it goes into there and that's a vortex chamber.

Discs, drains and vortexes? Is this new teenage speak?

Mike: And it goes into the B filter which is like a pool filter and it goes out through a UV sterilizer which kills all the algae.

Now, meet the Koi Boys.

Devin: We run it, we do all the day-to-day operations, catching fish for people, feeding Koi, we do all that.

They are teenage importers of Koi, a Japanese fish with a yen for swimming into money.

Devin: She's got to float 15 minutes to get the temperature the same.

Ron Schara: Is it a male or female?

Devin: It's a female.

Ron: So, what makes this so valuable to the Japanese?

Mike: This is their show dog, yeah, or like show horse, or a thoroughbred racing horse.

Ron: So this is just for show.

Devin: We can probably let her go, it's been about 15 minutes.

Importing a large fish with a $4,000 price tag is nothing new to the Koi Boys.

Mike: We're the largest facility that imports from Japan in the Midwest.

We ship these all over the country too.

They're all similar, these are between $250 and $600. It's all based on size and pattern.

While Mike and Devin run the operation, their parents provide home schooling and financial help.

Mother: I'm very impressed with my boys, they learned at an early age if you want something your going to have to work for it and that's kind of spilled over into this business. They're good at raising fish, but they still don't make their beds or clean their rooms.

Father: Dealers always want to talk with me when we're in Japan, our translator tells them no, deal with the two boys, they are the owners, I'm the banker (laughs).

We're doing double what I thought we'd do, so the word is getting out. People are finding us, people come wanting to buy one fish and they end up buying four - just cause our quality of fish is so good.

For six hours a day, the Koi Boys tend to their finny treasures.

Devin: We feed 'em all day long. Over in Japan they feed 'em seven times a day in a heated tank.

Mike: I'm not really working, it's more just watching the fish, because everything is pretty easy to maintain in here.

Koi may live a century or more, an unusual lifespan for a fish.

Mike: The oldest one was 236 years old.

Once a year the young fish importers go to Japan to wheel and deal for more Koi.

Devin: Hopefully we can stay with it and make a lot of money and get a lot of good Koi.

Mike: I handle all the internet and all the paper work.

Devin: I do Koi health and stuff like that.

Ron: You seem like you guys get along pretty good.

Devin: That's just a show we put on (laughs).

Do the Koi Boys have future plans?

Devin: To be able to retire at an early age (laughs).

Importing a large fish with a $4,000 price tag is nothing new to the Koi Boys.

Floatin' The Mississippi
MISSISSIPPI RIVER

One day at a Chicago Sports Show, of all places, I met a pair of Minnesota entrepreneurs, Bill Plantan and Dave Frink, who had combined their **love of fishing** to create the perfect fishing canoe. In the years that followed, **our Minnesota Bound cameras took many float trips in that special canoe called the River Ridge.** One of my favorite journeys combined the historic upper Mississippi and a comfortable fishing seat in the **perfect fishing canoe.**

Ron's Narrative: Of all the fishing rivers in America, this one offers the longest ride. The Mississippi River. Two thousand, five hundred miles on the Father of Waters. Fishing partner Bill Plantan and I floated downstream like modern Huck Finns in a fishing canoe with all the bells and whistles.

Bill Plantan: We hang the electric trolling motor in the rear. Put up the solar panel plus the battery up front and presto, we'll have a charged battery all day.

This stretch of the Mississippi, upstream from Minneapolis/St. Paul, is a hangout for smallmouth bass.

Bill: Holy, moly, popcorn, batman. A big fish just jumped right over there.

River smallies are to rocks and rapids what leaves are to trees. They're never far apart.

Bill: The smallmouth bass has been described by Earnest Hemingway as inch for inch, pound for pound, one of the fightingest fish in the sea.

When the leaves turn, when geese use the Mississippi as a southbound route, a smallmouth bass puts on the food bag.

Bill: One of the beauties of fall fishing is the way the temperature affects the fishing. When the temperature drops below 65 degrees, smallmouth bass become more active. Winter is coming and it's time for them to start eating.

Today anglers on the upper Mississippi are fighting hard to protect the smallmouth from over fishing and an encroaching suburbia along the river banks.

Dave Frink, River Fan: I've grown up on the Mississippi and I absolutely love it! We have to protect such a valuable place.

And it all starts at headwaters of the Mississippi River. The Mississippi begins its long run in northern Minnesota at a wild and scenic setting amid big pines known as Itasca State Park. In the park, school kids can brag about walking across the Mississippi. Early explorers didn't have it so easy. Nobody could find the headwaters until a man named Henry Schoolcraft came along.

River Historian: Henry Schoolcraft had the wisdom to ask a local Indian for help. The Indians brought him to Itasca and showed him the start of the river.

The river begins its long journey — wild and fishy.

River Historian: When people think of the Mississippi, they think of big and ominous and barges. They think about lots of boats. But up here at the headwaters, there's nothing but natural river.

Downstream, the Mississippi slowly grows tamer. With more lawns instead of trees. Only the fishing action showed no signs of surrender.

Bill: Oh, there we go – there we go. I got a walleye. I was sure that was going to be a smallmouth.

Wherever the Mississippi turns and bends, it's a sportsman's paradise. Bridges and barges may taint the atmosphere, but the river's lunker walleyes don't know they're living in a city.

River Angler: Fishing on the river you get a little of everything – from freight trains to helicopters. But if you can catch big fish in the Twin Cities who cares?

Downstream from Minneapolis/St. Paul, the Mississippi grows tamer and tamer with locks and dams to tame its current. Until you get to Cajun Country at the mouth of the Mississippi in Louisiana.

Meet Peter Vado. Peter is a Cajun to the core. He used to fish and trap in the swamps along the Mississippi.

Peter Vado: I was doing that seven days a week – rain, cold, nothing could stop me. I used to love to do that – my old lady said I did it too much. I say no, not too much.

There's a 55,000 acre swamp near the end of the Mississippi River.

It's a place where duck hunters and trappers roam.

Cajun Hunter: Down here, coots or water chickens are called a French word, "poulet." Along with ducks, wild turkey and deer – lots of deer, they live in the cypress swamps along the river. Plus you're apt to look eyeball to eyeball with mosquitoes or even alligators. In other words, it's an outdoor paradise.

So, the Mississippi ends as it began. The Father of Waters. And forever a place to enrich our lives.

And it all starts at headwaters of
the **Mississippi River**. The
Mississippi begins its long run in
northern Minnesota at a
**wild and scenic setting
amid big pines known as
Itasca State Park.**
In the park, school kids can brag about
walking across the Mississippi.

Joy of Lake of the Woods
LAKE OF THE WOODS, MINNESOTA

I don't remember the exact moment, but through the years I fell in love with a **14,000 island** paradise known as Lake of the Woods. While the lake's history has included ups and downs, there aren't many lakes with such an endless mystique. Truly, you could fish Lake of the Woods for a lifetime and **never fish the same spot twice**. But I'm working on it.

Ron's Narrative: Once upon a time, where the muskie swims and makes broken hearts, there was a fisherman who fell to the charms of Lake of the Woods.

Ron Schara: Aaah there he goes (releases the muskie).

This is a love story.

Neil Robertson, Fishing Guide: It's the world's greatest lake. It's got everything in it. Muskies, northern, largemouth, smallmouth, crappies and it's one of the best walleye fisheries in North America.

And so aptly named. Lake of the Woods includes 14,000 islands and a watery maze that straddles the international border between Minnesota and Ontario Canada.

Guide: The thing that keeps me hooked on it is trying to learn my way around it. It never ends. There's always a new hole, a new point, a new weed bay. You couldn't cover it all in a lifetime if you lived to be 150 years old.

The reason this is a classic walleye lake is because it has such an abundance of bait fish. And it's a lake with weeds, rocks, reefs, everything the walleye needs is right here.

If you were to write a script for what's perfect about a lake, Lake of the Woods fills the script. Anything you want its got.

A special Lake of the Woods treat is a fresh walleye shore lunch prepared by guides from Wiley Point Lodge.

Chef: It's lemon pepper on walleye – this is what it's all about.

A fish dinner to dream about. Somewhere amid the islands of Lake of the Woods, there's another dream. A dream fish.

Ron: I'm gonna cast and cast and cast – this is muskie fishing man. This is like waiting for a stick of dynamite to go off. You never know where he's gonna appear. You are on some of the class waters of the world. Although muskies are not any easier to catch, you've got a chance for a fish of a lifetime. That's the magic of Lake of the Woods.

Guide: It takes a lot of persistence and perseverance. A lot of people fish a long time before they get their first legal muskie. But cast long enough and sometimes you get lucky.

Ron: There he is – there he is.

A muskie brings on weak knees but wide smiles.
A few minutes later, a 42 inch muskie brightened
the end of my fishing day.

Go rest my muskie (fish releases). We'll court again
another day in this Camelot called Lake of the Woods.

Field Trip Location

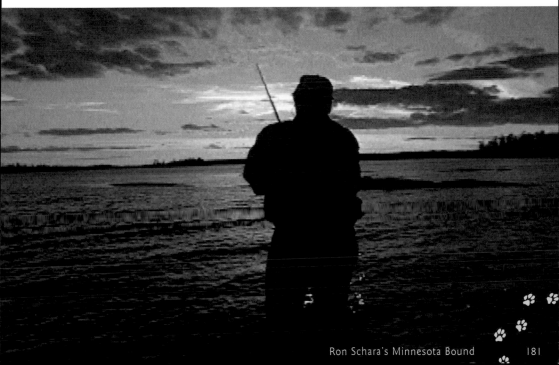

Joy of Opening Day

How could an outdoor television show in Minnesota ignore Opening Day?
No way. Opening Day is special. It means Minnesota as much as the Iron
Range. I once wrote that Minnesota has three holidays, Thanksgiving,
Christmas and Opening Day. We don't win Super Bowls in Minnesota but
we fish together. I also wasn't planning on writing verse for this story.
But — like a fish bite — it just happened.

Joy of Opening Day
Our fishing days are adawnin'
so how could you forget.
Start casting with the sunrise;
and quit when sun doth set.

They say we go afishin'
to land a meal or two.
But there's more to fishin' than catchin';
it's the other things we do.

It's boats and stuff, whatever you think.
It's safety vests for all.
Remember your rules on the water,
it's all common sense, you recall.

Your trailer may need attention,
the lights always need to light.
Remember grease on the axle hubs;
make sure you grease 'em right.

Boat numbers must be up to date,
if game wardens pass you by.
And skip the booze when you're fishin'
or it's you the law will fry.

Your minnows must be lively,
to catch that wily walleye.
So keep 'em happy and swimming,
or they'll belly up and die.

Remember landing nets,and lures
and hooks, and trolling in the deep.
You dream of monster fish below;
that's why you're losing sleep.

Now, fish don't care who's holding the pole,
or how you spell your name.
Fish don't care if you're rich or poor.
Your luck depends on your game.

For proof let's look at our leaders,
our governors who party and such.
They fish for our votes on the Opener,
but they seldom ever catch much.

Yes, fishing might be fishing,
and catching lights the way,
But you don't have to be a pro angler,
to appreciate Opening Day.

So here's to you and your friends,
who love the thrill of the bite,
who gather for Opening Day every year,
and the world again seems right.

Larry's Hunt for Big Fish

While Minnesota boasts of its 10,000 lakes, we seldom brag about the folks who fish those 10,000 lakes. In fact, Minnesota is home to some of the **best freshwater anglers in the country**. Among them, the Lindner brothers, Al and Ron; Gary Roach; Ted Takasaki; Doc Sampson; Ted Capra; Al Maas; Larry Anderson; Muskie Doug Johnson; to name a few.

There is only one Minnesota angler, however, who may have the credentials for the title best angler in the world. Meet Larry Dahlberg. Raised on the St. Croix River, Larry over the years has worn many fishing hats from **tackle salesman to lure inventor**. Through it all, however, he was always a fishing zealot. Some years ago, he developed a new fishing concept for television that struck at every angler's heart, a hunt for big fish. Larry's Hunt for Big Fish has taken him around the world in search of big fish in freshwater or saltwater. And nobody gets 'em bigger.

Ron's Narrative: If there's such a thing as the best job in America, Larry Dahlberg may have it. His task? To hunt for big fish.

Larry Dahlberg: I've caught some real good ones right here.

Truth is, Larry Dahlberg has caught good ones all over the globe. And that's no fish story. You've seen Larry Hunt for Big Fish on his ESPN 2 television show with the same name.

Ron Schara: What are you throwing now?

Larry: A crank bait. A friend of mine in Alaska gave it to me. He said it was a good luck charm.

In Larry Dahlberg's world, to catch a bass as big as a mailbox, you have to fish smart.

Larry: You have to stay one step ahead of the fish. Because they learn. This is the equipment room – this is ground zero.

The lures I use on a daily basis are here. This is the A-team. The first line of defense is right here.

If you look real close there might be teeth. Piranhas often leave teeth. In fact, the first time I fished 'em, I was throwing a bait like this, he hit it, came up and spit it out, and there was a tooth sticking in it.

Ron: Your name is on lures, so you've invented some lures.

Larry: Flies primarily. I've invented all kinds of lures but I don't share them with the world.

Ron: What kind of flies have you invented?

Larry: The most popular one or the best known one is called the Dahlberg Diver. And it's a fly that floats on the surface and when you pull it goes, bloop, bloop, bloop,

But lures don't just bloop, bloop, bloop by themselves. A fishing addict since boyhood, Larry took his first guiding job at age 11, growing up on the St. Croix River near Grantsburg, Wisconsin.

Larry: I don't know exactly what happened. But as a little kid that's what I wanted to do. Not make a career, I just wanted to catch 'em.

Following stints in various fishing businesses, Larry in 1993 launched his television idea about everybody's fishing fantasy.

Larry: I just thought it would be a good idea for a TV show, go catch big ones instead of all these little ones – big is better.

Today Larry lives with his wife, Marilyn in a hilltop home overlooking the St. Croix River Valley.

Ron: You have a whole cabinet full of memoirs here don't you?

Larry: Yeah, there's a lot of stuff around here.

Ron: Tell me about some of this, what is this here.

Larry: This is the skull of a fish that lives in the Zambezi and in the Nile called a Tiger fish.

Indeed, the world is his favorite fishing hole.

Larry: I've made 23 trips to Africa since I started doing this. All fishing, some 30 days long, fished freshwater, saltwater and both continents, it's an amazing place.

His fishing memories go around the globe.

Larry: In 10 days once we caught 18 blue marlin over 600 lbs. I'd never fished for 'em in my life before. Biggest was 1,300. Up here in Lake Nasser, I would love to go there again. If I had one week to live that's where I'd go. Clean, clear water, no humanity and fish that look like smallmouth and weigh over 200 lbs. You wanna come with?

While fishing is Larry's game, including a calendar full of fishing trips, casting is not all of his existence.

There's also playing. The man who catches big fish also happens to be a big guitar picker. What kind of music? Fishing songs, of course. About unusual trips.

Larry: I've been in 3 revolutions, one in Venezuela, one in Bom Bom Island and I was in Red Square May 1, 1993. That was a little scary.

Ron: Have you ever had any guns pointed at you?

Larry: Oh many, many, many guns. Oh yeah, because they got 'em and I don't. One of the times it was about midnight and I went outside to take a leak and I hear this 870. This guys got a stainless steel 870 with full camo and tells me his name and explains he's never been defeated in battle and I'm sitting there you know "Can I zip my pants up?"

But, says Larry, fishing the world is getting tougher in other ways.

Larry: Our ability to harvest fish from the ocean commercially as a human race, has exceeded the ocean's ability to create and replace those fish. And it's been going downhill since 1986.

But his boyhood river, the St. Croix, still delivers fish when Larry makes a cast for smallmouth.

Larry: It's a nice one. He's really pulling...(fish splashes). I love these guys. It's a different deal. When these guys bite, it just proves that you're alive and everything is the way it should be. Boy, he really ate it...Isn't that a gorgeous fish? Look at how fat he is.

Ron: Just when we thought we weren't going to catch anything.

Larry: I never doubted for a minute.

So, yes, big fish are still biting for the man who hunts 'em. And the good life for Larry Dahlberg is still a tight line.

Ron: What would Larry Dahlberg do differently in his life?

Larry: Oh, I'd have retied a couple of fishing knots.

A fishing addict since boyhood, Larry took his first guiding job at age 11.

Meet Mr. Ice Fisherman

MONTICELLO, MINNESOTA

Most anglers carve out a reputation by catching a bunch of big fish, or winning a bunch of money in fishing tournaments. Still others write books or star in their own television shows.

David Genz did none of these things, yet he's as famous as any Minnesota angler. Dave's passion and expertise was for winter fishing — staring at a hole in the ice. Nobody stares better than Dave Genz.

Ron's Narrative: In the sport of ice fishing, mystery swims under the ice. While above the frozen waters, time seems to stand still. Welcome to the world of Dave Genz.

Dave Genz: Good luck out there. Catch a big one.

When its wintertime, it's time to meet America's ice fishing guru. He's an angler extraordinaire who from Maine to Minnesota has become a celebrity, inventor and entrepreneur of ice. And he catches fish.

Dave: This one's not little.

As you might expect, there's no place else he'd rather be than fishing in a hole in the ice.

Dave: I like fishing. And in a one person shelter, you can sit inside and it's just me and the fish.

For almost six months of the year, Genz seeks enough ice for safe fishing. He heads to Canada in late fall wherever there's ice thick enough to walk on. And his winter season doesn't end until the ice melts. Along the way he catches fish, promotes ice fishing equipment and makes a full – time living as an ice fishing specialist.

Dave: My dad was a road construction worker so he didn't work in the wintertime and many times he'd go 30 days straight and go ice fishing every day. My dad used to scratch his head all the time because when I was young, most of the time I'd end up catching the big ones.

Prior to his ice fishing career, Genz worked as a maintenance man for a laundry company, fixing boilers and steam pipes. In his off hours, he worked on his ice fishing inventions, including a small, portable fishing shelter. It became a quick hit in the market.

Dave: What's nice about the fish trap is it's easy to set up, you just get to your spot, just pick it up and flip it over top of you and you're inside here where it's warm.

More ice fishing innovations followed and suddenly Genz was the ice man.

Ice Angler: Dave is the master of ice fishing actually. He's really revolutionized ice fishing as it is today. I think the more time you spend on the water the better you're going to be and with Genz – there's no question about it.

Jeff Arnold, Ice Angler: Dave Genz is our hero because he went ahead and took his knowledge and taught people how to catch more fish and enjoy a sport. That's why Dave Genz is the Michael Jordan of ice.

Today, not forgetting his ice fishing roots, Genz passes on his passion to a younger generation.

Dave: Ohh there's one on there, already. Small one but there's more down there.

It's the moment when they catch their first fish or actually figure it out and you see the excitement in 'em and you know you've made them a fisherman for life.

This one's pulling a little bit harder. Now, that's a nice perch.

Big fish, little fish, big kids, little kids. It doesn't matter. To Dave Genz, happiness is a hole in the ice.

Dave: It's part of the peace and quiet. No phones ringing, no eye contact with anybody, I can just sit there and concentrate on catching the fish.

And nobody does it better through a hole in the ice.

...and suddenly Genz was the ice man.

Meeting Muskie Tom
LAKE VERMILLION, MINNESOTA

Of all the anglers I know, the strangest ones all fish for muskies. **The fish makes 'em that way, I suspect.** While we've followed many muskie casts in hopes of filming a strike or massive catch, it seldom happens. So, when I suggested a story about Muskie Tom, my camera crew wasn't convinced. Turns out, Muskie Tom was quite a character. **He also has earned his name.** You want to catch a muskie? See Muskie Tom.

Ron's Narrative: Sooner or later, if you venture to Minnesota's Lake Vermillion, you'll hear about the one and only Muskie Tom.

Muskie Tom, whose birth name is Tom Wehler, is seriously stricken with an angling disease called muskie fishing. There is no cure. But it helps if you live on Lake Vermillion, hunkered on a small island, and living in a small cabin that is stuffed with muskie lures and other muskie paraphernalia. It's not Wayne's World; it's the world of Muskie Tom.

Muskie Tom: About ten years ago, my wife Bonnie named me Muskie Tom because I was kinda obsessed with wanting to be the go - to guy on this lake. And everything I did was to collect muskies, read about 'em, and spend all my time on the water trying to find out why they do what they do. Which was basically about where to find them, when and why.

Living on an island surrounded by muskies was perfect.

Muskie Tom: I always wanted an island. No neighbors, no one on that side bothering me, or that side. I worked in the city for years. It's a little too much for me, for what I want to do right now. I like this. And I go back in the winters – I can handle that. Everyone is shut in and then I can have the city to myself.

Of such obsessions are muskie anglers made.

Muskie Tom: There's a mystique about muskies. I don't know why. They're not an easy thing to catch. It is very challenging and it is very visual. And it's very rewarding when you get one.

Muskie Tom's idea of fun is to cast and cast and do it again and again.

Muskie Tom: I'm a little bit different, but I know what I'm all about. I keep things simple. Try to not sweat the small stuff. Enjoy life. A lot of people leave this life in your lifetime and no one has ever come back to tell me any different. You only get one shot, so go for it. Enjoy today for what it is. Try to have fun.

In truth, Muskie Tom's fun never ends. A decade ago, he quit the usual work world and launched his own fish guiding business.

Muskie Tom: I thought I'd try it. I was doing really good, I was having several four fish days, and taking friends out and putting them on fish. I've always guided for pop or beer money, gas money, stuff like that.

You don't get rich in the guiding business but his office address is priceless.

Muskie Tom: It's just absolutely beautiful. It's breathtaking at times. The sunsets are unbelievable. It's very quiet. There's an abundance of wildlife. The lake seems to go on forever and from any corner you can see something different.

Amid hundreds of islands, cabins and houseboat vacations on Vermillion, Muskie Tom has new fishing partners almost every day. Today, it's a fellow Minnesota muskie addict, Tom Mackin, and Rapala Fishing Pro, Mark Fisher.

Tom Mackin: Muskie Tom, I gotta say, he's one of the most colorful characters I've ever had the opportunity to fish with. It's kinda nice, we can talk rock 'n roll and we can talk pro hockey, he's a true Minnesotan! But he knows this lake – he knows it like the back of his hand.

John Denver once sang. Some days are like diamonds; some days are like coal. It's perfect muskie fishing music – most days are coal.

But not with Muskie Tom. Unbeknown to Tom Mackin, he was about to cast into one of Muskie Tom's diamond mines. A muskie in excess of 50 inches, the largest muskie of Tom Mackin's fishing days, soon was preserved in memory and released to fight again another day.

Tom Mackin: He's forgotten more about muskie fishing than most people will ever know. He knows the spots. He knows how to work the spots. And the thing about this is – it's such a big lake with 365 islands that all look like good muskie water, especially if you haven't been on the lake. It takes a guy like Tom to say, ok, these are probably the most productive spots and eliminate some of the dead water right away.

Muskie Tom: You meet really good people on the water, and a whole variety of 'em. And I like teaching people what I know how to do and what I've learned to do.

Of such are the life and times of Muskie Tom, the muskie guide. Another day brings another bout of muskie fever, a fever with endless optimism.

Muskie Tom: You're only one cast away from having a very, very successful day.

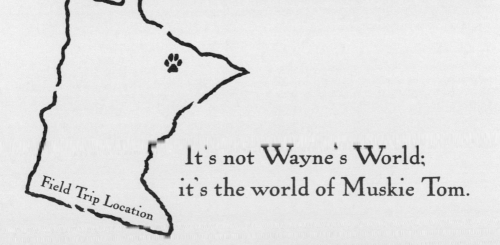

Field Trip Location

It's not Wayne's World;
it's the world of Muskie Tom.

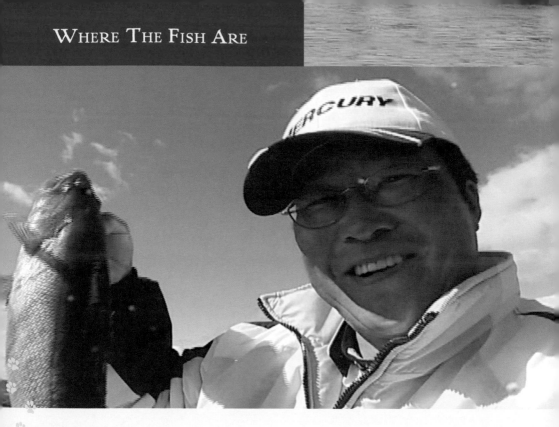

Ted's Fishing Tale
BRAINERD, MINNESOTA

When I first met Ted Takasaki, he was a young angler from Illinois who worked for a high-tech company. He so loved fishing in Minnesota, his idea of a **weekend drive was 600 miles** or more. Time passes. Ted wanted to be a good walleye angler. More time passes. The next thing I know he's a **world champion** and then...Ted really lands **the big one.**

Ted Takasaki: It's pretty out here isn't it?

Ron's Narrative: For Ted Takasaki, a day of fishing on Minnesota's Rainy Lake is always pretty nice.

Ted: What color did you start with Ron? Chartreuse and green? Everyday is a new challenge you know? These are living critters that move around and have their own preferences just like humans.

Ron Schara: Come on fish.

Ted: Marking some fish right here.

There's one, you just never ever get tired of that feeling, oh yes, nice walleye. Gorgeous, living gold right here.

Ron's Narrative: In the game of fishing, Ted Takasaki has made the biggest catch of his life. It was a catch the pro angler never weighed in any walleye tournament. It was a catch that never made the family's picture album. It was a catch so big that, frankly, Ted Takasaki never expected to land.

Ted: I am probably the luckiest guy alive.

You see, Ted Takasaki is one of those rare anglers in America who went fishing and caught...well, he caught his dream job.

Ted: This is where I spend a lot of my time right here. This is the hub, where everything gets done.

Ted's dream job is president of Lindy, a national fishing tackle company based in Brainerd, Minnesota.

Ted: We just reconfigured everything here, and are buying new shelving and taking all of our packaging up a little higher.

I tell you what - there's nothing better, to be around fishing my whole life and everyday I enjoy coming into the office. Being out in a tournament or in the office I enjoy both aspects of the business.

At Lindy, thousands of hooks, lures and floats are made and shipped by dozens of employees who require a boatload of decisions to be made every day.

Ted: I enjoy everyday, I look forward to the next day, and I look forward to a year from now, so I'm often very optimistic and passionate about what I do.

Passion, preparation and persistence are the 3 p's that are the mainstay of anybody's mantra per say.

Nevertheless, rising from an angling nobody to company president is an impressive fishing trip.

Ted: I started fishing when I was three years old. My dad and my mom always went fishing, we'd always fish on little local farms. We never had a boat so we'd stand on shore and cast out with bobbers and a sinker and a hook.

A former Illinois resident, Takasaki once was anchored in the world of high-tech sales and high pressure.

Ted: I think anybody who doesn't have a certain level of stress or pressure in their life becomes complacent.

But his dream job, fishing, never faded.

Ted: The American dream is to be able to get up, do what you love to do for a living, go back to sleep, get up and do it the next day. In America you can do anything you want to do, that's what's great about it.

Turns out, Ted loved catching walleyes. And the walleyes loved him. In 1998, Ted reached the top of the walleye tournament scene, winning a national championship.

Ted: I was named after Ted Williams. Ted Williams was my dad's favorite baseball player. My dad was a very avid fisherman, he loved to fish. He passed in 1989. If there's one thing that I wish, I wish he could be alive today to see me, where I'm at now because he would really enjoy it.

From a fishing kid to a fishing champion to a fishing president.

For many anglers, a fishing trip of a lifetime.

Ted Takasaki is one of those rare anglers in America who went fishing and caught...well, he caught his dream job.

Field Trip Location

Walleye Egg Magic
PETERSON STATE FISH HATCHERY, PETERSON, MINNESOTA

To a Minnesota walleye angler, the most important event in nature takes place in April. It's the annual spawning run of walleyes. In some places, Minnesota DNR workers intercept those spawning fish to collect the eggs to be hatched under safer conditions, a state hatchery. The walleye egg collection process made a good story for us. It also **elevates the heart** of any living walleye zealot.

Ron's Narrative: This is Minnesota's version of a gold rush. Golden walleyes, rushing to spawn, rushing by the dozens to someday fulfill every angler's greatest hope.

Angler Spectator: I'm dreaming (laughs). I'd like to put a little locater on these and follow them. I fish here quite often, and have never caught one like this yet.

But these walleyes in Minnesota's Pine River, are spawning...with a helping hand.

DNR Hatchery Man: We usually do two females to each male. So we'll put the eggs of two females in a bowl, and go with one of the males. There's a hog! Look at that! Just look at the eggs in her.

DNR Man: What we're doing now is stripping eggs out of the walleye. That walleye is about 14 to 16 years old. She probably has about a quart and a half of eggs in her. That's equal to around 200,000 eggs.

Since 1906, Mother Nature's spring spawning ritual has been sidetracked by DNR fisheries workers. The DNR has trapped walleyes to strip them of their eggs which are then manually fertilized by milking males of their milt or sperm.

Having the DNR duplicate nature's handiwork is all about fishing, of course. That is, having more walleyes to catch.

DNR Man: Well, you know, Minnesota's favorite fish is walleye. It's the state fish, this operation and nine others are extremely important to that mission of providing walleyes for the angler.

Every spring the DNR collects enough eggs – upwards of 700 million – to raise roughly 250 million walleyes to stock in lakes with no natural reproduction.

DNR Man: About 90 percent of the fish that are caught in the state come from natural spawning populations in the big lakes. But this program expands the walleye fishing to medium to large and small lakes throughout the state of Minnesota. There would be very little fishing, especially in those lakes without natural reproduction, if we didn't stock walleyes.

Angler Tourist: I think it's fantastic. It makes me think that my grandchildren are going to be able to catch walleyes.

Indeed the walleye gold is handled with care. Each female may produce 125,000 eggs.

DNR Man: We don't take all the eggs. These people have been doing this for many years, so they know what they have to do. They release the fish, and they go upstream, and presumably continue to spawn. And then eventually they go back down into the lake.

The collected eggs – now fertilized – go a different direction. To a DNR fish hatchery where some 80 percent may survive. In the wild the survival rate is less than 3 percent.

DNR Man: And this incubator is what hatches the eggs. They'll be in here three to four weeks, depending on how the water temperature rises. Eventually you'll see the eyes, and that's when we call them "eyed eggs."

Three to four weeks later, the eggs magically turn into tiny walleye fry ready for stocking. Years later and if all goes well – the walleye egg becomes an angler's wish.

Why I Fish

Why do I fish? It's a fair question but it's not an easy answer. For one thing, we anglers are seldom asked to explain what keeps us casting, keeps us hoping to catch something. It's no mystery to us. Perhaps the only people who are puzzled by fishing are those who don't do it.

It's been said the essence of fishing is much more than casting or retrieving or playing your catch. It's the wind in your face, they say, the sound of awakening birds as the sun peeks over the horizon.

In every fishy place there is magic and mystery, of course. And the quest to unlock the secrets takes you to some of the world's garden spots. And let's not forget the pure joy of catching — that moment when a fishing dream is on the end of the line. Memories are made of this.

Fishing is also a teacher. And the lessons learned in a fishing boat are not lost on land, either. Patience is a big teacher. Patience is required. But patience pays.

To fish is also to be humbled. Not once but time and again. Frankly, lessons in humility help keep life itself in perspective. Sure some of us tend to exaggerate a fish or two, it's said. But for every tale of giant whoppers there are the true stories about the one that got away.

There's also an eternal side to this pursuit we call angling. It's a pursuit of a lifetime.

You're never too young to start. And you're never too old to quit fishing. And I like that. As my own Opening Days wind down to a precious few, it's nice to know I'll be there as long as I can. As long as I can bait a hook and make a cast. As long as I am living. I'll be fishing.

Wild About Walleye

To most Minnesota anglers, happiness is something flopping on the end of the line. If that something is a walleye, the mood turns to euphoria. It's like hooking gold. A golden fish with a golden taste. In a frying pan, the walleye is the filet mignon of fishdom.

In Minnesota, there's more good eatin' swimming in more water than any other state. Almost 2,000 lakes in the state are home to walleyes, walleyes naturally hatched or raised in a dozen state — owned hatcheries. Every spring state fisheries gather upwards of 700 million walleye eggs.

Walleyes are even Minnesota's official fish, declared so by the state legislature back in 1965. But there's more to this golden fish than golden fillets.

A walleye is not a pike, although some folks say walleye pike. It's actually a member of the perch family. It's a fish of the night. Those big marble eyes gather light for nocturnal forays. In the spring, it spawns at night. It takes roughly four years for a walleye to reach the size of 1 pound.

Minnesota's record walleye weighed more than 17 pounds, but most anglers are happy with 10 pounders. Heck, most anglers smile for two pounders.

Walleyes are also good sports. The fish will take live bait, such as minnows and such, but it'll also inhale artificial things like leadhead jigs, spinners and different whatchamacallits.

Maybe the nicest thing about the fish is where the search for walleyes may take you. It might be a first class lodge with all the trimmings including modern boats and fancy meals. Or the hunt for walleyes might take you into wilderness waters where home is a rustic cabin and the air carries the songs of loons.

In the summer wherever there's good walleye fishing, you'll also hear the sound of happy voices. Anglers happy to be alive, happy to be catching walleyes, happy to hear the sizzle in a pan. When it is time for shore lunch. It's a meal of euphoria — fresh walleye.

Walleyes are also good sports.

A Day with Ted Nugent

JACKSON, MICHIGAN

The first time I heard Ted Nugent speak about hunting I was disgusted. Whack and stack 'em? What kind of hunting manner was that, I wondered. Then one day I got to meet Ted Nugent during a South Dakota pheasant hunting trip. I confronted Ted and asked him if his message was hurting or helping hunters. We talked and I learned that Ted's message was blunt but also very honest. Hunters are conservationists. If you don't like it, go soak your head in your own garbage.

Following our meeting, Ted invited us to his home in Michigan to discover the real Motor City Madman.

Ron's Narrative: On stage, you might remember him as the Motor City Madman. His is a rock and roll act with animal music. Wild as a zebra. A lion king with a guitar. He has growling hard rock hits like Cat Scratch Fever and he's sold more than 30 million albums worldwide.

But off stage, there is a different Ted Nugent. He's a family man, a grandfather on a different stage. It's also deer hunting season in Michigan. It's predawn and Nugent is in his favorite mode: camouflaged and jawing about hunting. As dawn nears for another day of deer hunting, it is Nugent's favorite moment, a sunrise.

Ted Nugent: I happen to think a man's sexuality is determined by the number of sunrises he lives. It's all about the spirit. Someone has to tell the kids that dragging your lazy ass out of bed this early has its rewards.

To Ted Nugent, hunting is what's right about America. While Nugent's rocking guitar made him a star in the late 1970's, Nugent credits his love of an outdoor lifestyle for sparing him from the fate of some of his peers, the likes of Keith Moon, Janis Joplin or Jimmy Hendrix – all dead from drug use.

Ted: They would literally ridicule me because I wouldn't smoke their dope. Meanwhile Jimmy got high and Jimmy's dead. I went hunting and I'm still Ted.

Today, Nugent never misses a chance to preach the same message to his rock fans. No booze, no drugs.

Ted: If you really want to get high, go hunting a white-tailed deer. It'll make you a better student, a better cop, a better teacher. I was gonna say better lawyer but there's no hope for them.

Nugent's been described as a pony tailed combustive rocker, law abiding hunter, lifelong anti-drug and alcohol crusader and a right wing gun toting grade school father of the year. He leads that life with his wife Shemane and son Rocco. Inside, the Nugent household is adorned, not with musical memories, but stuffed critters.

Ted: I'm comfortable in the presence of dead stuff. There's no question about that.

Shemane says her husband's hunting urges are the perfect balance to his high energy rock concerts.

Shemane: I think hunting is what pulls him back to earth.

Hunting is also Ted's obsession. And his enemies are anybody who opposes hunting, especially politicians and animal rights supporters.

Shemane: He does what he does for nothing because he loves to hunt. It's part of who he is and he is gonna do it forever.

Almost daily, Nugent is interviewed on rock stations. He eagerly preaches his hunting message and pounces like a cat on his critics, rock fans or rock stars. Not everybody in the hunting community supports Nugent's brash in-your-face style but he's not bothered.

Ted: I gotta tell you I get great joy out of causing that discomfort.

Nugent believes his way is reaching America's youth.

Ted: See there are four seasons: Spring is when stuff starts growing. In the fourth season – winter – stuff dies. Season number four can only support half the wildlife that summer and autumn supported. Therefore, if you don't harvest – that is – kill the surplus and use it with some respect, it will all go to waste and rot.

Nugent is convinced the battle for public opinion over hunting will be won by common sense.

Ted: Americans have no problem with dead stuff. They eat it on a daily basis. They know it was a pig or a chicken or a turkey or a cow, a small cow, a pretty cow, a cute cow and they don't honestly give a damn. It's a cow. It's dead. It's food. Next.

To **Ted Nugent**,
hunting is what's right
about **America**.

All About Antlers

A scientist might describe antlers as merely calcium deposits atop the skull. And that they are. But nothing explains our long fascination with antlers. Hunters and non-hunters alike will stop and pause at the sight of antlers. Some folks collect antlers — others hunt them in the spring as if the dropped tines were as tasty as morel mushrooms. Over the years some sets of antlers have been so coveted they were stolen, whisked away like fine art by an antler thief. Our fascination with antlers shows no signs of letting up, of course, which is why we did this story. The more we know about antlers; the more we cherish those who have them.

Ron's Narrative: This is a story about antlers. Of all the wonders that grow on earth, one of them certainly is antlers. Antlers on deer, on elk, on moose, and on caribou. Each antler an original – a one of a kind – no set like another. And don't mistake antlers for horns. You find horns on cattle or cape buffalo, even rhinos. But horns and antlers are not the same.

Unlike horns, a new set of antlers grows every year starting in late spring. A thin, fragile velvet-like skin, rich in blood vessels deposits bone-like calcium and...presto...antlers.

Truth be told, antlers are all about sex appeal. Come fall, the male deer rub off the velvet, revealing an ornament of bony branches – a crown if you will, all to impress females and intimidate male rivals.

Yes, antlers are a male thing, except for caribou cows. Yes, cow caribou have antlers. Go figure.

Although you can't tell an animal's age by counting the points of an antler, males in their prime tend to sport the largest antlers.

So trophy antlers take time. A buck whitetail needs 5 or more years to develop an exceptional rack...bull elk 10 years to reach his antler peak.

Big or small, there's something about antlers that captures our fascination. We create record books for record antlers. We hang antlers on our walls. We even turn them into things like lamps.

Antlers oh antlers.
You grow so divine.

Yet mystery surrounds
Every antler design.

Like when do they branch
Or grow a new tine?

If men were like male deer in the rut in the fall.
We'd all want big antlers to make us look tall.

But be careful what you wish for.
When you answer such a call.

Your head and your antlers
Could make somebody's wall.

Boys on Main Street
PARKSTON, SOUTH DAKOTA

I've always admired folks who are passionate about what they do. In this story, we happened on three Minnesota pheasant hunters who so loved to be on the prairies of South Dakota in the company of Ringneck pheasants that they bought a house. On main street. In a small South Dakota town. This story turned out to be more than just three fellas who hunt birds. They had become part of the community. They knew just about everybody. They even loaned their house to local folks who needed extra rooms for family gatherings. No longer were they just autumn visitors or crazy nonresident pheasant hunters. They were the boys on main street.

Ron's Narrative: Once upon a time in the small country town of Parkston, South Dakota, there was a house on main street that nobody wanted. Then one day, three pheasant hunters from Minnesota wandered into town to meet an old friend.

Butch Hawkins: Patty comes along and says I think you can get a house for three. For three? Thirty thousand, I don't think so. She said no, three thousand, and I said what? You can get the 2 story house with 4 bedrooms, wooden floors, cut glass windows and full kitchen.

Skip Hall: I thought we were absolutely crazy. Cause why would we need a house when we could stay in the hotel down the street for 20 dollars a night.

Butch: Then Patty comes in the door with a big smile on her face...you got it! We were the only bidders (laughs).

So begins a story about the boys on main street...Skip Hall, Butch Hawkins and Gerry Brouwer. It's a story about big city boys living with small town folks. All because of South Dakota's famous gaudy game bird – which binds them all together.

Butch: Hi neighbor.

Neighbor: They're good neighbors, you don't know they're around when they're here.

Oh, when pheasant seasons rolls around in October, the house on main street starts jumping. Guests arrive. Hunting dogs bunk where they want.

Skip: It's kinda an open door policy and we have enough space, if it gets overcrowded we roll the sleeping bags out on the floor.

Butch: There's the syrup.

Skip: How you make it is how we like it! Eating has never been a problem here.

Butch: Everybody else gets to cook, so I do the dishes and that's fine with me.

Gerry Brouwer: It's absolutely effortless, we all enjoy the same things, there are no issues. I went to school with Butch and ran track against Skip. We maintain a sense of humor and we know each other so well that, number one, you know which buttons not to push.

Their days are spent rousting Ringnecks. And it's a passion they share with their dogs.

Butch: C'mon Trigger, c'mon bud, good boy.

Skip: Easy come! There's a rooster right there...nice shot Ron. Get the bird, boy it didn't take him long to get the bird. Good retrieve there.

Their hunting passion extends to South Dakota.

Skip: I have come here since I was 7 years old. Shot my first pheasant at 8 years old with a 410 double barrel.

Butch: South Dakota started...47 years ago when I was 12. I've only missed one year and two openings...one I had pneumonia...and the other my daughter was born.

Gerry: Well, it's the guys...the hunting is fun and everybody's got dogs and as you know spending time with your dogs, that's the fun part about it. Watching them work the fields.

Out in the country there isn't a farmer they don't know. Yet pheasant hunting never comes with guarantees.

Butch: And they're the Wiley Ringneck – and they are named that for a reason. Because we haven't figured them out yet, and I don't think we ever will.

But there's another side to living in Parkston.

Butch: Once you know everyone in town it's just like putting on an old glove.

Gerry: You'll find that this is middle America, these are nice people, they're kind, they're genuine, there's no pretension at all out here and that's what's fun.

Skip: We have friends here and when they're getting married, we come out here as we would for anybody else.

Gerry: You know everybody in the town...and everybody in the county, and everybody is nice.

So – that's the way it is for eight long weekends every autumn. Minnesota boys on main street in a South Dakota town.

Butch: No rules...just have fun.

Fun in Parkston, South Dakota. Population, three more.

These are **nice people**, they're kind, they're genuine, there's **no pretention** at all.

Elk Hunt in the Snow

CRAIG, COLORADO

If timing is everything, once in awhile you get lucky. I've taken many elk hunting trips over the years but always in early autumn when the Popple leaves turn to gold and bull elk bugle from on high. One year my elk outfitter friend, Dick Dodds, suggested a late season elk hunt. Dick promised that such a hunt would be different and would make a good television story.

Unbeknown to Dick or me, timing and luck were about to come together. A few days before we arrived, the Colorado mountains were hit by the season's first heavy snow, which triggered a massive elk migration to lower levels. We happened to arrive at Dick's Elkhorn Outfitter's camp on the same day that thousands of elk marched out of the high country. Despite camera problems, videographer, Mike Cashman, managed to capture the unique moment in nature as well as our hunt on the backs of mules.

Elk Guide: (whispering) We've seen some elk just over the hill here so what we'll do is we'll go over here and we'll sneak up and see if we can see any bulls there.

John Hauer: Do any good to call 'em?

Elk Guide: Well, we'll have to wait and see if we need to. We might try a cow call and see if we can bring 'em down and we'll just look at the situation.

Ron's Narrative: It's late autumn in high country near Craig, Colorado. Snow has come with a promise that more will fall. For elk hunters, this is the season of harvest.

Elk Guide: They're in that brush.

My friend John Hauer and I have come to Elkhorn Outfitters in Craig, Colorado where the peaks reach for the moon. It's the kind of country made for a mule. Dick Dodds, owner of Elkhorn Outfitters, once a horseman, is now a mule believer himself.

Dick Dodds: Mules can handle about any kinda riding we have on our ranch from the 10,000 foot to 6,500 foot. If you need to cover long distances they're there. If you need to go up and down steep country, they're also there to do the job.

Dodds' goal at Elkhorn is to provide quality hunting. It's another reason why every morning his horses or mules are being saddled.

Dick: The main reason we did it all on foot and horseback was because we wanted to put the integrity of elk hunting back in the hunt. It's not that truck hunting is bad. It's just that sometimes elk hunting on horse makes you feel a little bit better. That's real hard to explain because it is just part of hunting being on a horse and trying to outwit an elk and follow what they do.

A former flatlander from Minnesota, Dodds started Elkhorn Outfitters and began guiding elk hunters more than two decades ago.

Dick: Our place is unique because we can hunt in September with a rifle in the rut so most of our hunting is done up high. The September hunt is a lot more riding and bugling; the herds aren't as big but it's more of an intense type hunt. You'll hear one bugle and you'll try to figure out which way the wind is going. Then you try to either bring them to you or you go to them. Later in the elk season, we move down in the 7,000 to 9,000 foot range. We still hunt on horse or mules but its mostly a spot and stalk hunt.

When the elk start migrating depends on the weather. Generally in the first to third week of November, they'll travel 50 miles or more. For the elk, themselves, the promise of deep snow in high country triggers one of nature's great migrations. And when it snows in Colorado's high country, it snows, and snows, and snows some more. For as long as mountains have been high. For as long as snow has covered them, herds of elk – not by twos or fours, but elk by the hundreds, have instinctively left their high summer range to escape winter.

Dick: My personal belief is that there is a lead cow somewhere in that group that will just keep moving. Her calves follow and then pretty soon all the bulls follow the cows. Some of these cows might be 10 or 11 years old and they're passing off to their offspring the migration route. It's not an easy migration. Fences, highways, towns and hunters make it a tough road.

To watch this massive movement is to be humbled. And to think it almost disappeared is to be angered.

By 1920 in America, the elk were almost gone. Wiped out by unregulated hunting. Today, elk herds are thriving in America, thanks to limited seasons and hunter financed elk management efforts. By 1970, elk populations had grown to 500,000 animals. Today, elk numbers are closer to one million animals.

Dick: The best part of the late season is the wildlife that you see when you're hunting. Earlier in the year you'll see elk here and there in smaller bunches, but this time of year you'll see herds of 1,000 to 1,500. There have been days when we've seen 3,000 or 4,000 elk in one day.

With elk marching like herds of cattle, its fair to ask – is an elk hunt under those situations closer to an elk shooting gallery? Dick Dodds has the answer.

Dick: The only thing I want us to be known for is that our quality means everything and our integrity in hunting is everything. We can go kill elk like nothing flat but if there isn't some meaning in somebody's hunt then it's for nothing.

As I follow Guide Dick Dodds, an elk hunter soon comes to the realization that nothing is ever easy about elk hunting. And that's probably a good thing.

Dick: Right over there we've got to keep the wind in our nose – we better stay on top – if we don't stay on top then we're going to lose them in the brush.

But elk have a way of disappearing.

Dick: What happened to those cows that were up on the side? Where'd they go?

With no answer, you climb back into the saddle and ask your mule to do the impossible. I'm riding Sassy. John is aboard Honey Bee and Dick is on Ambrose.

Another trail. Another climb. Snow is falling like a white sheet. But nothing seems to bother a mule.

Dick: There's a bull down here — boy they picked a good spot to bed down in. I think they're down below us someplace.

Ron Schara: I think he is too.

Dick: Here comes a nice bull coming over the top — there's that bull now. Look at him coming through the top. Big bull.

We knew the elk were close but they knew we were close, too. Suddenly what began as a slow stalk, turned into a frantic slide through deep snow — as we rushed to get into position for the shot.

Dick: The bull is on the top, he's on the top — see him up there?

Ron: Yeah.

Dick: Sit on your butt.

Ron: How far is it?

Dick: Hurry! He's coming up on the bottom — hurry Ron hurry! There he is on the top — the 4th one looking right at us. Ya got to take him — right there, take him Ron, take him, take him!

I squeezed the trigger of my 7 mm magnum Remington. My hunt was over. The bull fell. But even in death, a bull elk keeps its majesty.

Ron: How old do ya think this guy is?

Dick: He's probably 3 1/2 years old. Gosh he's got a big body.

My elation was as high as the mountains as my trusty mule carried me out of this theatre of elk. If only for a few days, I was witness to one of nature's magnificent and unforgettable moments.

Now I had two moments to remember...a bull elk and a trusty mule.

To watch this **massive** movement
is to be **humbled**.

A Miracle in Rochester
ROCHESTER, MINNESOTA

Most folks who visit Rochester or go to the Mayo Clinic are unaware that a conservation success story hangs out downtown. These are the Canada Geese of Rochester. There's lots of them. In Silver Lake Park, they'll eat corn out of your hand. When the same bird flies out into the country, you can't get close to one. But these are special Canada geese for one big reason. They are giant geese. A half century ago, scientists thought the giant Canada goose was extinct. Well, guess what.

Ron's Narrative: The busiest city park in America may be here at Silver Lake in downtown Rochester, Minnesota. While the Mayo Clinic made Rochester famous, these geese are kinda famous, too.

Back in 1962, biologists discovered a miracle. A giant Canada goose, which was considered extinct, was found living in downtown Rochester. And not just one giant, lots of giants.

Gary Quandt, Goose Hunting Guide: They say we peak at 35,000 in the fall. All total, some 75,000 will fly through depending on the winter and temperatures. We've had as many as 30,000 stay in Rochester all winter and as few as 8,000 stay.

There's enough geese now that every autumn, the outskirts of Rochester go from suburbs to hunting fields.

Gary: Most people decoy the birds and there's about a dozen outfits in town. Some with guides for hire, some without.

But these downtown birds are not dummies.

Gary: They know where the refuge lines are. They know the whole routine. The birds we are hunting are all pretty educated.

I tried goose hunting for a few hours but most of the geese simply flew overhead, high and safe. If I wanted a close look at a goose giant, I needed a new ploy.

Mark Schoenmann, Goose Guide: You can go to Silver Lake and feed the birds out of your hand. Soon as they leave the city limits they turn into a different animal.

True, but a goose hunter can change, too. Instead of hunting for a fat goose, I bought a bucket of shelled corn to make a goose fat.

So, I never pulled the trigger that morning, but I had the Rochester geese eating out of my hands.

These geese are kinda famous, too.

Of Elk and High Country
COLORADO ROCKIES

If you ever hear the bugle of a bull elk, you'll want to hear it again. It's a contagious sound in a contagious place. All of which explains why another of my passions (too many to count) is to pursue elk with bow and arrow when autumn comes and a bull elk sings to the mountaintops.

When you cherish something, you want to share it. So you're invited along to hear the bugle of the bull.

Ron's Narrative: It's late September in the Colorado Rockies, a place where autumn arrives early. Mountain sides of once-green Popple almost overnight turn into glimmering vistas of yellow and gold. In high country, wild flowers quickly become victims of autumn's chilly nights, but the flowers of summer hang on, clinging to their blossoms, and offering one last pit stop for a hungry monarch butterfly on its way south.

Yes, Colorado's Rockies become magical mountains in September. Not only by what you see. But also by what you hear. The bugles of bull elk. Native Indians called them wapiti. By any name, the bull's bugle is a sound unmatched in nature. And in September – the mating season, the bull's whine, grunts, bawls and screams ring from the peaks and echo down the valleys. Elk cows sound like a cat when they call to a bull. But in the hunt for elk, some cow calls come from two legs, not four. Outfitter Dick Dodds, of Elkhorn Outfitters, in Craig, Colorado has been hunting and calling elk for more than two decades.

Dick Dodds: Of all the cat and mouse games between man and nature, this is the fall classic. Calling bull elk into bow range. Sometimes it's real hard to explain. You share something in a real short time that not many people get to experience.

Ron Schara: Do you remember the first elk you saw?

Dick: You bet, just like it happened yesterday. Who can forget such moments?

Suddenly a bull elk stepped into view. He checked the wind and ambled cautiously toward Dick's cow calls. Minutes seemed like hours. Would the bull walk into bow range? In the next minute, we got our answer. This bull chose caution over companionship and slowly disappeared. We'd try again tomorrow.

Ron: Some September mornings are almost magic. Elk music fills the air. I'm surrounded by elk as Dick calls.

Dick: Man, he ain't very far away. Cows will come first and then it will be him Ron. He's gonna come right into that opening right there. Just pick your shot.

This cat and mouse game was heating up.

Dick: Left Ron, left. Get ready, get ready.

My arrow never flew. Just another close encounter of the elk kind. This time the elk's nose detected us and quickly our morning hunt was over.

Dick: We need a little luck, Ron.

Dick Dodds started Elkhorn Outfitters two decades ago as wildlife manager for more than 100,000 acres of ranch land. His hunting lodge has all the essentials – good food – good company and lots of hunting stories. To improve the quality of his hunts, Dick also changed his hunting style. Instead of 4-wheel trucks, he now leads his hunters on friendly horses to reach elk country. Not all riders have horse sense, of course.

Ron: When I get on a horse, Dick, it's poetry in motion.

Dick: I see that.

Our horse train takes us on a ride into the elk's world. Dick Dodd's affection for the animals became evident as he pointed to elk sign. And his eyes were uncanny at spotting any animal. As we rode and walked, Dodds knew and I knew a successful bow hunt for elk was no easy made for television experience. When you're bow hunting for elk you're faced with two sets of special problems. One, of course, is to get close enough to the bull elk and by close I mean less than 40 yards preferably 20 yards. Another problem is, will the bull turn broadside and present a shootable target.

Late one morning, while Dick made cow talk, one bull bugled back to us and sounded serious about coming to the party. Suddenly, he was there. Less than 20 yards away. But deep in brush with only his nose in view. Close enough but no shot. My arrow stays put. But the moment was a reminder of the elk's magic. It's a memorable meeting with things wild. It's revisiting your own instincts and senses it's hiking unblemished landscapes and discovering natural wonders. But the hunt wasn't over. The end of another day was near when, suddenly, an unexpected encounter.

Dick: There's a bull elk in the trees over there. Get behind that bush.

Dick began calling. Quietly I wait, bow drawn, arrow ready. The king of the mountains is getting close. My mind races. Playing the role of predator is an emotional moment for me. And, I suspect, my brother the wolf feels the same. Any hunter does.

Dick: It's like putting all your emotions in your hand at one time.

A hunter learns that the joy of success is never guaranteed and the pain of failure is always possible.

Dick: A bull elk is one of the tougher things you'll ever chase in your life. They are one of the most beautiful things you'll ever see in the wild and one of the most beautiful things you'll ever hear when they're bugling. And they live in beautiful country.

When the day ended, my hunt was over just like it began. There would be no success story. What I bagged was something called hope. Hope that future hunters will be able to enjoy what I've been able to enjoy. Septembers. Mountains. And the bugle of bull elk.

It's like putting all your **emotions** in your hand at **one time**.

Remembering the Swamp Boys
TALMOON, MINNESOTA

For many autumns, there was an annual gathering of friends to celebrate fall fishing and grouse hunting. Many fun and memorable times were had. Dogs were welcomed like members of the family. We called ourselves members of the swamp. Years later, the owners of the swamp had to sell. Today the members still gather but without the swamp and it's just not the same.

Ron's Narrative: When autumn comes and a changing sunrise turns the green maples of summer into October's gold. It's time to go to the swamp.

The swamp? Bill Rosso's wife named the place.

Bill Rosso: She came and looked at these cabins one day and said why did we buy this. She said its nothing but a swamp. From that time on, it's been called the swamp.

Wives don't show up at the swamp very often, but the rest of us do. We call ourselves swamp members. As gatherings go, it's an annual but unusual event held in the Popple thickets near Talmoon, Minnesota.

Gary Amluxen: Well, the swamp is a hunting club made up of lots of dogs and quite a few people that have known each other for quite a few years.

Duane Boyle: It's a nice place to go because there's no telephones and it's very relaxing.

Al Beisner: This is a very rare situation, I believe. I don't know if we could ever duplicate it.

Bill: It's a very bonding relationship we have. We do it once a year only.

Stalking the wily ruffed grouse is spoken here. And everybody shares their stories.

Lee Felicetta: Aaah we did not do great. We walked a lot.

If the grouse is cherished in the swamp lodge, grouse dogs are treated like family. Rocky is the only golden retriever at the swamp and likes to play the role of pest dog. Rocky is the only male dog in the swamp.

Rudy Froiland: Rocky come here. Rocky get out of the way. Rocky leave that dog alone.

Four-legged or two-legged, at the swamp there's no shortage of characters. And everybody remembers the night the wolves almost knocked at the door.

Duane: We heard 'em at night. After the cocktail hour we started howling back at the wolves and they answered.

There's a thousand stories at the swamp. And Lee Felicetta is one of them. Nobody pounds the grouse trails like he does.

Lee, Swamp Co-Founder: What really attracts me to grouse hunting is that it's a solitary sport. The thing that excites me the most is when I get a flush. That gets the adrenalin going more than anything else. I'd rather go out and have 25 flushes and not shoot any birds than shoot one bird.

Most swamp members feel the same.

Lee: I've got a special fondness in my heart for it. I've had some of the best times of my life there. It has been a wonderful spot.

Maybe that's the spirit of the swamp. Memories. Friends. And the swamp finale? A banquet of grouse breasts.

Al: It's white meat. It's pure. And we fry it in pure butter.

John Beard: It's the filet mignon of the woods. If the rest of the world only knew, there wouldn't be any grouse left.

Good times, as is always the case, tend to end too soon. On the last day, the swamp class of '97 gathered for a last picture. There's Bill. And Don. Todd and Jeff, Al and Lee. Plus John, Rudy, Gary, Duane and me.

God speed, swamp friends.

Grouse dogs are treated like family.

Why I Hunt

This short television essay came about because I wanted to explain why I hunted — or at least try to explain — because I knew that a growing segment of my television audience included more folks who didn't hunt than those that did. While hunters in America have a conservation history to be proud about, hunters have been generally lousy at telling their story. Most of the hunting shows on television today tend to emphasize the glory of shooting that big buck or dropping wily mallards. Seldom do viewers learn why America has so many deer today or why mallards still fly over the land. I also wanted folks to know that, regardless of their views about hunting, the experience of hunting is important to the quality of my life. And nobody can argue about that. The question is easy; the answer is not.

Why do I hunt?

What do I smell in the autumn air that a growing number of Americans do not.
To me, the fall season means hunting.
For most Americans, it means football.
There was a time when Opening Day attracted hunters far and wide across the rural landscape.
Now we are mostly urban dwellers whose connections to the land and its wild game are fading slowly away like the last light of day.

The last hunting season of the 20th century bears little resemblance to the first.
Near the turn of the century, hunting was unregulated and excessive. And wildlife populations almost disappeared. Today hunters follow seasons, limits and the rule of fair chase.

Only about 15 million Americans call themselves hunters these days.
And we ask ourselves why.

Doug Smith, Outdoor Writer, Minneapolis Star Tribune: Well, it's a
hard thing to explain. It's more than just going out there hunting. To me,
it's the sights, the sounds, the smells.

Maybe words and pictures can't convey the personal nature of hunting?
One answer to why we hunt may be because we always have.
Like the wolf, we, too, evolved as predators with canine teeth.
Yet, our hunting motives seem to go far beyond those of a wolf.

Do I follow my dog, Raven, to hear the rush of wild pheasant wings? Or
feel the rush of my heart? Do we wade in marsh muck and hunt the sky to
fire a gun? Or to lift our spirits with the majesty of waterfowl?

To hunt the white-tail deer is to discover — and yes, love — the animal's
grace and guile. These are instinctive gifts not seen in a petting zoo. Did I
say love? To be a hunter who loves the hunted is its own puzzling paradox.

But it is real. America's hunters have left a remarkable legacy of wildlife
conservation. More deer. More elk. More antelope. More wild turkeys.
America enjoys more wildlife in more places.

The wildlife success stories were paid for by hunters through license
fees or contributions to wildlife organizations, such as Ducks Unlimited,
Pheasants Forever and the National Wild Turkey Federation. Hunters
have been putting their money where their heart is.

That's love, isn't it?
And that's why I hunt.

Tribute to the Ringneck

One of the most successful wildlife introductions in America is the Ringneck pheasant. If it has habitat, it thrives in the Midwest Cornbelt. I can still remember the first Ringneck that fell to my .410 when I was a boy. I also remember a bird that I missed. Any bird that can tweak such memories, deserves a story of its own.

Ron's Narrative: It's the Beau Brummel of birds. Feathers richer than gold, with cherry red cheeks and a raucous cackle unmatched by anything else that flies. From the Dakotas to Kansas, from the prairies of Montana to the farmland of Minnesota, the bird's golden hues are as much a sign of autumn as the turning leaves of oak and maple.

These are the joys of the Ringneck pheasant. And the bird, we can thank an Oregonian judge, a fella named Owen Nickerson Denny, for. Denny imported the first Ringneck pheasants from China back in1880 and let 'em go on his farm. They thrived. Minnesota released its first Ringnecks in 1905 and three years later South Dakota had its first successful stocking – a few dozen birds.

By 1940, South Dakota was home to millions of wild Ringnecks and claimed the title, pheasant capitol of the world.

Rancher, Cody Warne: They just thrive in South Dakota. They call 'em cocky roosters for a reason – they are cocky.

Today this oriental import has become an icon for rural Americana.

Veteran hunter, Bob Summerside: He's a smart intelligent bird. A lot of people think that a pheasant is easy to shoot, but I've kept hunting records over the years, if you shot 60 percent your doing good.

Our long love affair with pheasants also means we don't want a shortage, either. The world's largest pheasant grower, McFarland's pheasant farm in Wisconsin, pumps out pheasant eggs and pheasant chicks at a rate of more than one million birds a year.

Despite incubators and bird pens, the Ringneck's place in America has never been secure. Intense farming practices and land-use changes constantly threaten the bird's survival.

Joe Duggan, Pheasants Forever: In Minnesota, we're down to about 1 percent of the entire prairie that was originally here.

Since 1982, Pheasants Forever, a national conservation group has worked to preserve pheasant cover by changing federal farm programs and working with landowners. More than 115,000 members across America now work to keep pheasants and pheasant hunting alive and well.

More than 100 years now have passed since this feathered immigrant landed, but our infatuation with Ringneck pheasants, shows no signs of waning. Author Steve Grooms explains why.

The Ringneck, Grooms wrote: "Is courageous, wily, brassy and unpredictable. And beautiful. Too damned beautiful for words."

Today this oriental import has become an icon for rural Americana.

Ode to the Whitetail Deer

Please don't confuse me with a legitimate poet. Writing poetry is not my calling in life. And I shall be the first to admit that some words don't fit. But there have been times when, faced with writing a Minnesota Bound script, I was struck with poetic license.

This ode to a whitetail was one of those times. The words just appeared.... much like the gray ghost of the woods. Now if any poets are deerly offended by my rhyming skills, the buck stops here.

When autumn glows under the rutting moon, this is your time ol' friend of mine.
You, the whitetailed deer.
Your beauty is forever awesome.
Your grace is nature's best.
I never tire of seeing you, ol' friend of mine.
You, the white tailed deer.

They say these are the good ol' days for you and your kind.
You roam not only the forests but the fields and farms, too. There was a time when this century began, you were almost gone. Now we've got you coming back to 20 million strong.
Now you're plentiful, and sometimes a pest crossing a road.
But still a pretty pest,
You, the white-tailed deer.

And here's to you ol' big horned buck. You're royal sight, a majesty
in antlers.
You're the fantasy of every deer hunter in the woods. And that includes
me ol' friend of mine,
You the white-tailed deer.

Since time began, you've been the prey; I've been the predator.
For a million years we've played these roles.
While I made you and you made me.
Today some say the game should end. That you're too pretty to be hunted
down. They say against me you can't defend. Yes, they're talking about you
ol' friend of mine,
You, the white-tailed deer.

But nature's law cannot
be changed.
Its been the hunt for you that
gives you grace.
It has made your feet so fleet.
Your eyes and ears so good.
Your nose so fine.
You survive because you've
been hunted.

If the world will listen I'd like to say,
Every autumn its an honor
And a challenge and a privilege,
And I'd like to make this clear.
To share the woods with you ol' friend of mine,
You, the white-tailed deer.

A Turkey Nut Like Me

I've been a turkey nut so long, I'm actually tired of talking about it. So, you can imagine my delight when I met Dick Alford. He was a nut case just like me. Maybe worse. Wild turkey nuts make great stories, of course. It also gave me another reason to write about the great American birds that make some of us kinda crazy in a wonderful way. I think.

Ron's Narrative: He looks normal enough. And he talks normal enough, too. But Dick Alford is not normal. He's a turkey hunter.

Dick Alford: He's going over the hill, no he's still standing there.

The he in turkey hunting is a wild tom turkey. Otherwise known as a gobbler. And it's also the reason Dick Alford is nicely a nut case over turkeys, toms or hens.

Dick: Oh she's digging...that's a good picture (laughs). She digs it up looking for worms...worms or grubs...I think she's gonna come up here.

Wild turkeys seldom do what you think. Maybe that explains why Dick Alford, a retired teacher, turned abnormal over turkey hunting a quarter of a century ago.

Dick: I finally got a bird permit in MN in '80 and I started traveling. Two states weren't quite enough and then I was hunting 5 or 6 states and been doing that ever since. I've hunted in 16 mainland states, New Zealand, and Hawaii.

It's so exciting for me to hear a gobble – when the bird comes in and it's successful, it's a real thrill. My hunting partner John Hewitt said that when he got his first bird he let out a primal scream and I guess I'm not screaming anymore, but I'm still excited.

But Dick Alford's turkey addiction doesn't end when the hunt's over.

Dick: C'mon down Ron, watch your step, this is where I have most of my hunting gear.

Alford's woodsy home in Minnetonka, Minnesota has walls of turkey this and turkey that.

Ron Schara: Look at the beards (Laughing).

Dick: I have beards in the drawer and on the table and I put them on a stick.

Ron: What a cool room if you like turkeys and other stuff. Tell me about this turkey over here – he's got quite a distinguished spot in your room.

Dick: Well that boy was shot in South Dakota – it's a long story, but he had 3 beards and at the time he was ranked as 5th – 5th best Merriam in the country.

While hunting tom turkeys in springtime is Alford's primary passion, what does a turkaholic do the rest of the year? In Alford's case, he takes his turkey fever on the road, giving how to fool 'em seminars at events like Minnesota's Game Fair.

Dick: These guys are secretive, they don't join with the big flocks and you have to settle with a Jake for the year.

Between seminars and making turkey sounds, Alford has found time to write books about turkeys or invent turkey calls to sell to fellow turkaholics.

Dick: I came home from golfing and I didn't have a lot of luck that day and I had the golf pencil on the table and a shotgun shell and I just tried the piece of wood, and it wouldn't make a sound and then I pushed it in there and finally figured out if I push the lead in there it would make a sound (demonstrating the prototype).

Dick: I've sold over 900 sets of strikers.

When he's done making purrs and putts, Alford makes turkey jewelry.

Dick: This is a series of spurs, a 15 year-old necklace out of parts of the leg, breast beads and hairpipes and it's a little trademark of mine I wear at banquets. I make turkey leg knives with the spur connected and a lot of other little things.

Alford says his wife has learned to tolerate his room stuffed with turkey knick-knacks.

Dick: I asked her (his wife) do you want to go to Hawaii next year? And she said, "I'd love to go." There must be turkeys there and same thing with New Zealand, there's turkeys too.

Ron: Would you tell anyone don't get into this, it's too addictive?

Dick: I've been asked that before. If I got a turkey last spring, I am still addicted now, and you might be too because once you get into it – if you stay with it – it gets in your blood.

And one more thing; turkey hunters never are normal again.

Wild turkeys seldom do what you think.

A Turkey Tribute

It is the bird that says Thanksgiving. Waddles, beards and all.

Historians say Ben Franklin championed the wild turkey as the nation's national emblem. Wild turkeys, Franklin argued, had higher morals than bald eagles who ate dead fish. Congress, however, voted for the bald eagle.

Ron's Narrative: In truth, America wasn't very kind to wild turkeys. When the 20th century began, wild turkeys were down to a few thousand. Minnesota's last wild bird disappeared in Rock County in 1871. Wild turkey dinners were an endangered meal.

Eventually, however, America discovered its conservation conscience and three decades ago, Minnesota reintroduced wild turkeys into the state's southeast forests.

Gary Nelson, Turkey Trapper: They're smart; they're really wary and it's difficult to capture birds. Number one, we have to locate where the birds are and get them in an area where they'll hopefully be isolated for awhile.

Once trapped, the birds are checked over and released in new habitat. For a wild turkey, it's been a historical flight. Today, wild turkeys are thriving in Minnesota and thousands of Minnesotans now enjoy hunting for their own Thanksgiving dinner.

In fact, turkey addiction is sweeping the country. Conservation organizations such as the National Wild Turkey Federation, raise millions for turkey habitat projects. The bottom line is America's woodlands once again harbor the beauty of a native bird. Forty-nine of the 50 states now have enough turkeys to warrant a hunting season. Only Alaska is turkey-less.

That brings us back to Thanksgiving. The boom in wild turkeys. It is something to be thankful about.

America's woodlands once again harbor the beauty of a native bird.

Florida Turkey Nap
BIG CYPRESS RESERVATION IN SOUTH FLORIDA

When you have an addiction, your life can become terribly complicated. This is true of drugs, of course. But it's also true of wild turkeys, which happens to be my addiction. This happens in April, which also happens to be the month I was born. My loving wife has spent more than 35 years with me but I don't think I've been home with her for more than five of my birthdays. This should explain why one spring day I found myself in the swamps of Florida, feeding my body to mosquitoes, while in pursuit of wild turkeys.

Ron's Narrative: First light in a Florida swamp. Hungry mosquitoes ring my face and hum for blood. I call for a gobbler's attention. He flies down…Never to be seen again.

Ron Schara: Did they just answer me?

Lenny Ray Jim, a Seminole Indian Guide: Yeah, the last time you called – they are over there. There's another opening right around this corner.

Ron: That's where they're at?

Lenny: Yeah.

Hunting the wild turkey. An eternal addiction. And, yes, I'm hooked.

It might be springtime in this Florida swamp, but to my Minnesota skin, it's hotter than an August sidewalk as Lenny, my Seminole Indian Guide, listens for gobblers.

Ron: Probably better move huh.

Lenny: Sounds like a plan. Let's see if we can find a lonely bird.

We turkey nuts relish these Florida swamps because every spring, it's the site of America's first turkey season.

Lenny: We got some more fields over here we'll go check that out.

Ron: Ok.

Lenny: Ready for some hiking?

When you're hot to scratch your turkey itch, you're willing to sweat in Florida.

Lenny: We call the wild turkey in the Seminole dialect, fahdit, which means a turkey. We call a gobbler turkey, fananoshi, that's basically saying old turkey.

Lenny Ray Jim is a top guide for a Seminole hunting service, headquartered at Billie's Swamp Safari in South Florida.

Lenny: It's an adventure in itself because you never know what these birds are going to do. One day they can run to your call and they can be gobbling at every call you make. Then the next day they're running from your call or they could be coming silently right behind you and you never know they are there until you're already busted.

Oh, I know all about wild turkeys and the mistakes I've made. I've been hunting turkeys in South Dakota and elsewhere for more than three decades. But Florida swamp turkeys, well, they're different. Just ask any turkey hunter.

Lenny: Osceola turkeys are a sub species of the wild eastern turkey and the Osceola turkey was named after one of our warrior chiefs that led the Seminoles into the Seminole Wars back in the 1800s.

Visiting Hunter: I believe that turkeys are turkeys wherever you go, but with the amount of calling that is involved, I'm probably doing it wrong here. From what Lenny has told me, Florida hens are pretty tight lipped where a South Dakota turkey hen will just chatter away 30 to 40 yelps in a row sometimes.

One morning after much calling, a gobbler answered but only a hen appeared. She raised our pulse and wandered away. As the sun rose higher into the Florida sky, the turkey talk went down while the temperature went up. By mid-afternoon, I thought I was hunting inside an oven. Uffdah – it was hot. Lenny decided we should set up along a sand road used by wild hogs and wild turkeys .

Lenny: In native tradition the wild turkey is considered a spirit because he can vanish so effortlessly. He can be at one point here and then you look there again and he ain't there any more.

Lenny you can say that again. There I was, sitting in the hot shade, and keeping one eye open for gobblers. Suddenly, I don't know when, both of my eyes went shut. My hen calls turned to slow breathing and loud snoring. Lenny was awake but not me.

Lenny: Psst, they are coming this way.

I never heard a word. There comes a time in every turkey hunter's life when the impossible happens, the unthinkable occurs and the unbelievable takes place. While I dozed, a flock of Florida toms waltzed into shotgun range, fluffed their feathers, pecked the ground and eventually vanished just like the Seminole legend said they would. My guide said he could only watch the birds walk away. Me? All I saw was the back of my eyelids.

It's an adventure in itself because you never know what these birds are going to do.

My Wild Turkey Confession
BLACK HILLS, SOUTH DAKOTA

I saw my first wild turkey **nearly 40 years ago.**
And I never got over it. To understand, you have to be in turkey
woods long before dawn. So, set your alarm. Here we go.

Ron's Narrative: To a turk-a-holic, the sight of gobblers strutting in the glow of the morning sun is like soaking up a bottle of free booze. It's a binge with birds. Allow me to introduce myself. I'm Ron. Vocation? Television host. Avocation? Unabashed turk-a-holic.

Hunting companion, John Hauer: Our addiction probably started more than 35 years ago when you and I started hunting together. We thought we knew what we were doing, but it was the turkeys who knew what they were doing.

For decades, my April days have been entwined with the mystique and magic of wild turkeys. And sharing the passion with others. Over the years, I've seen lots of folks get the turkey addiction at my turkey hunting camp, the Turkey Track Club. Our camp and the turkey makes strangers into friends immediately. My daughters Simone and Laura have their own turkey hunting stories, of course.

Simone Schara: The big question I have every April is will I go another season with my dad and not get a turkey?

Allow me to make a confession. As a veteran turkey guide over the years I've helped dozens of folks become successful turkey hunters. But when it was time to guide my daughters to a turkey I was like a novice. While Simone faithfully followed her father-guide through the woods, we couldn't get close to a tom turkey. On the other hand, her sister, Laura, needed only one morning to shoot a bird.

Simone: The only turkeys to come close to me were hens. Always hens. If we did see a tom, it was always in the next county.

Simone's warning rang in my ear.

Simone: If I go another year and there's nothing. I'm done.

I was down to my last morning. A tom turkey gobbled nearby. So close yet so far away. But then our luck changed.

Ron Schara: Wait until he goes behind the tree – scoot around a little bit.

Simone took steady aim and fired.

Ron: You got 'em, you got 'em!

Simone: I got 'em.

Simone's first turkey was worth the wait. A black hills beauty.

Ron: Now you get to carry him to the truck.

Simone: Holy hanna, he's heavy.

Ron: How much do you think he weighs?

Simone: About 50 pounds.

Ron: What do you think of turkey hunting now, Simone?

Simone: I'm a pro now.

Me, too, replied her father. Me, too.

For decades, my April days have been entwined with the mystique and magic of wild turkeys.

All About Being a Father

The secret to a good life, its been said, is enjoying the passage of time. In time that passage, for most of us, includes becoming a parent. In my case, a father.

Once a year in America, we celebrate fathers for being fathers. The idea of a Fathers Day, appropriately enough, was inspired by a good father. His name was William Smart. And he raised six children alone. In 1910, Smart's daughter, Sonora Smart Dodd organized a Fathers Day observance in Spokane Washington to honor fathers who are devoted to family.

Fathers Day became an official national holiday in 1972. So, happy Father's Day — fathers.

A day to call your own, a day to be appreciated is pretty nice to have.
But sometimes those of us who are fathers like to look at Fathers Day
in a different way.

I mean, we're the lucky guys.

Its been said, one of our duties as a father
is to teach our children all about life.
But fathers soon discover that our
children also teach us.
In time fathers also realize sons and
daughters are like gifts for happiness.

Oh, maybe, not all the time. Fathers and kids can have rough times.
Mark Twain said, when he was a boy of 14, his father was ignorant.
But when I got to be 21, Twain said, I was astonished at how much my
father had learned in seventy years.

The same is true of daughters.
I know. I have two, Simone and Laura.
Nobody told me they'd grow up so quickly.
Young girls to young ladies, just like that.
As a father, I should have known, but then
fathers aren't perfect.

Before it's too late, I've tried to share my outdoor experiences with
my daughters. Sometimes Simone is willing to fish with me. Sometimes
Laura is willing to tag along to hunt wild turkeys.
If they can't join me, I just wait for the next time.

That's because I've finally discovered that a father's greatest gift to his
children...is his time.

But fathers soon discover that
our children also teach us.

An Outdoorsman Celebrates July 4th

To some of us, the nation's birthday is more than parades and fireworks.
Oh say can you see by the dawn's early light.
So goes America's national anthem.
And we do. Sunrises. They touch our souls.

Is this still the land of the free, wondered Francis Scott Key?
In countless ways, Francis — countless ways.

Today our traffic may be jammed on July 4th holidays.
But we're free to hike a portage or carry our own canoe.
And we pitch a tent at our own pace.

We're free to float a river.
Or make a cast.
And free to wish to catch a fish.

In autumn in America, in farm fields and weed patches, there's more proof that our flag is still there.

Only in a free society do we go hunting carrying our own shotguns and calling our own bird dogs. While America certainly has changed since the first birthday, some parts of the land are still original.

Snowy winters in Yellowstone.
The granite shores of Lake Superior.
The wilderness of Minnesota or Alaska. Or wherever we find it.

On this Fourth of July, let us pause to remember our outdoor roots. Preserving and conserving America has been a tough sell. And it won't get any easier in the new century.

But succeed we must. And the world will know. America. It's still the home of the brave.

Floating Kodiak
KODIAK ISLAND, ALASKA

Nothing says wilderness adventure like Alaska's Kodiak Island. That may explain why I've returned to Kodiak more times over the years and for more reasons. My first visit was by boat in November in search of the island's Blacktail or Sitka deer, a close but smaller relative of the Whitetail deer. A second visit was in search of King salmon and close encounters with the island's largest resident, the Kodiak brown bear. If you ever want to swallow your heart — wade in a salmon river while in the company of the Kodiak brown bear. Truly, you are in the company of earthly giants.

One of my favorite reasons for going to Kodiak is to float its rivers in search of rainbow trout. A Kodiak river is like a ribbon of adventure that carries you through the essence of wilderness. Where red fox watch you fish like spectators; where eagles are as common as house sparrows; where you glide by the paths of the brown bear and view the splendor of an untamed land.

Ron's Narrative: It may not be the largest island in America but certainly it's the wildest. This is Kodiak. A towering chunk of granite surrounded by the North Pacific. It is not only a part of Alaska, it's a miniature version. Snow-capped mountains. Ocean bays rich in sea life. Untamed rivers, secluded lakes and only one way – by float plane – to get there.

This is Uganik Lake – It's a picture postcard full of fish. It is also our launching site for a rafting trip led by Alaskan Guide David Pingree and his neighbor John McCollough.

David Pingree: Boy did we luck out with a beautiful day – about as good as it gets. What you want to do today is what we will do today. And when you leave, you will leave a part of our family.

As rivers go, the Uganik is short, only six miles long. But it didn't take long to find the first rainbow hotspot.

David: In numbers, it's one of the best I know of, certainly the best on Kodiak. Size wise – pretty average, a 17-18 inch average today. But they are native, not stocked fish – just pure native fish.

Rainbows with a taste for a fly called a black wooley bugger.

David: All right Ron!

Ron Schara: Boy he slammed that thing. Oh, that's a beauty.

Our pattern was set. Catch a few rainbows or dolly vardens on flies or spinners and then raft on down to the next stop.

John McCollough: Ok Ron paddle-straight ahead – we want to get in this back eddy.

David: It's a nice stretch of water... Ron, see these big rocks right out here.

Ron: Alright! Fish on!

David: That fish has beautiful color – isn't he beautiful – just came out of the spawn. I just love fishing them – they're aggressive when they're feeding and they're beautiful fish – I wait all year to catch a rainbow.

Paula Foshay added a woman's touch. A pink salmon.

Paula Foshay: The challenge is to wade the strong currents and find the pools where the fish lie – you want to really understand the river.

Mile after mile, the Uganik trout played the fishing game. How many we caught and released? I lost track.

David: I never tire of it – I could stay here forever.

The only thing I take for granted here is eagles – oh it's another eagle. The rest of the land, the bears, the fish – you never get tired or take it for granted. And especially not the sun (laugh).

Did somebody say Kodiak brown bear? Our raft moseyed downstream in search of fighting rainbows and that's exactly what they did.

David: They are beautiful – they've got those spots, their color and they are good fighters.

We also learned something else about rivers on Kodiak Island. Chances are... you're not alone.

Ron: Trout rising, bears walking, heart thumping...(laughter).

A young brown bear stood on a nearby bank as we drifted close by. The bear obviously knew of our presence but chose to munch on grass and ignore our stares.

David: Bears are easier to live with than people – they are predictable. They are fun to watch, just real curious – and they'll keep their distance.

And David Pingree should know. Actually this bear is his neighbor. Not far from where the Uganik empties into the sea, Pingree lives with his wilderness family in a place called Quartz Creek Lodge.

Meet Pam, wife and mother. Then there's Levi, the youngest, Faith, not much older and then, Amy and then the oldest daughter, Beth.

David: I always wanted to come to Alaska – it was one of those dreams. And I joined the Coast Guard to come up here. I was stationed in Kodiak first thing and when I stepped off the plane – I said I love it and I'll never leave. And I never have.

It's a life of daily chores. Chores to gather food or care for the boats. As for fun, well, you make it.

Neighbors? Well, of course you have. Whales and sea otters. Nesting eagles and some weird looking fish known as the Irish Lord. But daily life for the Pingree family is no different from that of an oyster catcher. Their survival comes from the land or the ocean.

The nearest grocery store? A day's boat ride away.

David: It never gets old – it grows on you. Each season is different – you get to watch the eagles feed and it is just beautiful here.

I get more enjoyment watching other people catch fish than me. I just love bringing people out, sharing with them and watching them catch fish and have fun.

John: Just recently a fellow said to me, you know I'm a big talker, but I haven't said a thing all day because I am awestruck.

And it's contagious. When you catch Alaskan rainbows in the backyard of a wilderness family, that's what you become.

Awestruck.

Simply Awestruck.

A **Kodiak** river is like a ribbon
of adventure that carries you through
the essence of **wilderness**.

Minnesota Bound Christmas Tree

The gifts of nature are not
stored under a tree.
They simply light up our life
so wild and so free.

It's nature's bounty we harvest
including the tree.
Back to nature is a gift
for any time of year.

To catch a fish or drift a river
with friends we hold dear.

But nature is seldom perfect
she has flaws that others see.

That's why it's never easy
to find that perfect Christmas tree.

On this holiday season, look what we found?
it's a magical tree from Minnesota Bound.

Its branches are heavy with every outdoor wish
And ways to catch every catchable fish.

From the top with a prop, to a creel and a reel.
Plus an anchor in pine boughs and tiny fish that look real.

It's a Christmas tree of memories, of good times afloat.
With visions of lunkers in our little fishing boat.
It's a yuletide reminder of the fish that got away.
Of tiny flies and landing nets and fishing in a bay.

When Santa isn't busy, we know he likes to cast.
To anglers he brings a special gift, a true fish story that lasts.

A fishing tree is special too for the hope it sends our way.
The next Minnesota holiday a'coming is known as Opening Day.

So during this holiday season as you gather round the tree.
Here's a special heartfelt message from the dog, Raven, and me.

May all your catches be plenty; some big fish by the pound.

Happy holidays to you all.
From Minnesota Bound.

Saskatchewan's Living Sky

LITTLE QUILL LAKE, SASKATCHEWAN, CANADA

If your heart is into waterfowl hunting, when the autumn winds blow, there aren't many greater places to be than Canada's western prairies. This is duck and goose country — a historic gathering ground for birds as they begin their migration southward. While my heart has soared countless times at the spectacle of fall flights, this morning in Saskatchewan had special meaning. My daughter Simone, and Don Gonse, along with a special hunting friend, Mark Baker, CEO of Gander Mountain, were seeing the living sky for the first time. None of us will soon forget the dawn.

Ron's Narrative: The glow of another autumn day begins over Saskatchewan's vast prairie. It's late September and you're a goose hunter wrapped in a blind of willow shoots. Your eyes scan the sky. You've come in search of snow geese. You wait. But you really have no clue about the snow storm you are about to witness. It's an autumn blizzard in the sky that begins with just a white flake or two. Then more geese appear. A storm of snows on the rise. Until...it's a sky filled with swirling, feathered flakes. A squeal like a million clarinets. This is the September song of snow geese. And it's music for your heart.

Simone Schara: Oh my God.

A thousand birds? Ten thousand? A half million? At dawn and dusk on the autumn prairie, the birds are too many and the air too busy to count. They fly high with the clouds. They crisscross the sky. They gather in barley stubble and blow around like drifting snow.

Ron Schara: Oh my goodness. Hold your fire. Those are too high.

They pass above your willow blind. They look down upon your stone-faced decoys. And most of them keep flying.

Ron: You don't want to move till your ready to go.

But a few will fly no more. You're a goose hunter.

Mark Baker: Here comes a lone bird.

On this day each of us in our own way discovered something about the prairie. As Saskatchewan's themselves like to say – this is the land of the living sky.

Don Gonse: It looks like it's snowing – unbelievable.

Mark: Salt and pepper in the sky, huh.

Ron: Isn't that pretty, they call that slipping

Mark: I laid out in a stubblefield and I like doing that...because you are just facing up and watching the sky move from horizon to horizon. And your senses, I think, are very aware – you can hear them come from a distance and you really listen to the descending wings as they buffet back and forth. And that really is exiting to me.

Don: In the morning at sunrise, the sky is filled with ducks and geese – everywhere you turn it's ducks and geese. From as far as you can see, it's ducks and geese.

The living skies also may be too full these days. A population explosion of snow geese (including the blue goose) has led to liberal hunting seasons and limits to protect geese nesting grounds in the arctic.

Yet judging by the scenery on and over Saskatchewan's Little Quill Lake, the snow goose storm continues.

Mark: The sheer mass of them, when you see the first wave and then the second wave – You think it must be almost over now. And by the 50th wave, they are still coming.

Don: There were so many of them that I found myself getting overwhelmed. With all the geese in the sky to try and focus on one and to shoot one – a lot of times I missed them after everything (smile).

Snow geese by the thousands does not mean easy limits, however. Our willow blind surrounded by decoys pulled in a few birds until the morning light exposed our spot. With the morning hunt over, Hoosier the black lab was called on to sniff out the downed birds.

Later, as the wind picked up on the prairie, we tried pass shooting as the geese moved from field to field. With so many birds, geese were passing almost anywhere. Hoosier was watching. So were the rest of us. The truth is any place under the living sky is memorable.

Veteran Saskatchewan Waterfowler, Tom Brokken: It's beautiful communication once you get used to them, and listen to them, and to watch them. On a sunny day when they come into a lake – its just a million flashes – how they dip and dive – it is really exiting to watch.

A goose hunter on the prairie also learns something else.

Mark: It is moving all the time when you are looking at the sky. All morning long the sky is alive with movement.

And as you look skyward, as the birds wheel and churn, as the ducks and geese mimic a migratory flight centuries old, you feel something else on the prairie.

Under the living sky – you tend to feel mighty small.

This is the
September song of
snow geese. And
it's music for your
heart.

The Coming of Spring

Of all the changing seasons, autumn is the most colorful and winter
the quietest. But the changing season that most of us tend to miss
is the end of winter when the earth turns toward spring.

A robin in a treetop is the most famous sign of spring.
But in truth, the change to spring is more subtle.
Snowbanks retreat slowly as if the snow goes
away grudgingly, wanting to cover a landscape
that's still asleep.

Spring winds

herald the change of seasons and naked trees
seem to almost **dance with joy.**

Even water sounds happy as it drips and flows,
happy to be free from its icy state.
One trickle leads to another and to another.
Soon the water trickle has become a creek or stream.
Eventually from little drops, rivers flow.

Patience is a key when seasons change.
Some oak trees are in no hurry to drop their leaves.
Canada geese wait as couples for nesting chores to arrive.
While a woodchuck checks out the woods to see what's changed.
He's just awakened from a winter sleep that's lasted seven months.

Your time marches while seasons change.
Following spring, summer will come only to be replaced by autumn.
On her death bed, my mother told me, life goes on. For everything,
she said. From ducks to woodchucks...and for us, too.

The Joy of Sunrises

A rising sun. It may be nature's version of the greatest show on earth. And everybody in the whole world gets one every day. A sunrise brings us daylight. Sometimes warmth.

But almost always, **a sunrise makes us think.**

Rock star Ted Nugent once said, I happen to think that a guy's sexuality is determined by how many sunrises he lives.

Sam Cook, Nature Writer: A sunrise is full of possibility and potential and you're ready for whatever the day is going to throw at you.

Pat McManus, Author: The really great thing about sunrises is that they are free.

Ron's Narrative: Horace Mann said a sunrise is like a bracelet of time set with minutes made of diamonds. When it is gone no reward is offered because it is gone forever.

No two sunrises ever seem to be alike. An African dawn is certainly different when you greet the day with a giraffe.

Halfway around the world, a new day breaks over an Arkansas marsh and a symphony of birds wake up for a morning flight.

Sunrises in special places are always memorable. I watched the sun come up in Cuba one morning. Communism couldn't stop a rising sun.

All sunrises, no matter where, seem to shed light about life itself.

To author Jim Rohn a sunrise was a lesson in time. Time is more valuable than money, Rohn said. You can get more money but you can't get more time.

Sam: When you're up before sunrise and you're waiting for the sun to rise on a deer stand or wherever, you realize what a long process it is. You realize how slowly nature does most of what it does.

Ted Nugent: As that sun comes up, there's a stimulating growth of excitement, a growth of enthusiasm that happens in a wild setting and that nobody can sell.

Sunrises tend to be quiet times for most of us. We watch the break of dawn and bask in the silence. The most moving moments of our lives often find us without words, Marcell Marceau once said. Marceau was a mime.

Birds and beasts often greet the day in a noisy way, they seem compelled to tell the world about a new beginning on a daily basis.

To Mother Teresa, a sunrise was a message from God.

God is the friend of silence, she said, In nature, she said, trees, flowers and grass grow in silence. See the stars, the moon and the sun. See how they move in silence. We need silence to be able to touch souls.

Oh, some folks aren't fond of sunrises. Author Clifton Webb once wrote that he hated the dawn. The grass always looks as though its been left out all night, he said.

Rock star Ted Nugent thinks city kids especially should see more sunrises.

Ted: You've got sensations that ain't available at the mall, my friend.

Sam: You see a lot more sunsets than sunrises. But to me that purest time of day is the morning, and sunrises mean a lot more to me than sunsets.

Pat: When I was a kid camping out in the mountains at night, we'd lay there in the dark. When the sun finally came up and daylight returned, it was one of the greatest things I have ever seen.

Maybe a rising sun reminds us of a bigger responsibility. It's the start of a new day. One we can waste or one we can do good things with. When tomorrow comes, it has been said, this day will be gone forever; and in its place will be something you've left behind. Hopefully, it will be something good.

Let us all begin with.

Good Morning.

The most moving moments of our lives often find us without words.

The Magic of Autumn

Of all the seasons on earth, autumn in Minnesota promises
the most drama and delivers the loudest punch lines.

For these migrating geese, the sky's the stage; we earthlings
the audience.

Carl Sandburg, the poet, once said of autumn, I cried over
beautiful things. Knowing no beautiful thing lasts.

So even the most gorgeous leaves along Minnesota's gunflint trail
are destined to fall to earth. Almost everything comes to an end
when autumn ends.

Warm memories of summer. Summer flowers, too. They fade away like dear old friends.

Conservationist and hunter, Aldo Leopold, once wrote that all living things bring their unique contribution to the circle of life. And the key is to respect each.

That's especially true in autumn.
It's the season of harvest. For farmers. And for hunters.
The cooling air of autumn signals the start of nature's harvest.
From wild birds to wild deer.
For Minnesota's many anglers, autumn can be a time as magical as spring.
Fish remember to bite in autumn.

Longfellow wrote, the laws of nature are just, but terrible.
Yet, who can really find much fault with autumn?

Somebody once said the changing seasons is a much happier state than to be hopelessly in love with spring.

So let us be fond of autumn.
For, sadly, it is followed by winter.

Autumn in Minnesota
promises the most drama

The Wonders of Migration

Most of us were raised on robins being the first sign of spring. But robins actually are more than a sign. You might say **robins are a miracle of spring.**

Robins migrate. Lots of birds migrate. Some animals do too, such as caribou or elk. When you produce as much television as we do, you're always looking for a good story. Then one day, I saw a robin and, presto. We put together this story on migration.

Ron's Narrative: Some go by land. Others by sea. And those that fly take to the air. Migrating wildlife. For 3,000 years, historians say, we have watched and wondered about this natural phenomenon called migration.

And we still do.

Caribou Expert: In my own words I'd describe the caribou as a northern legend. These particular caribou in Manitoba come from hundreds of miles to the north.

Swan Expert: These swans had to discover their own migration routes because they did not originally have adults to follow.

Fish Expert (on Chesapeake Bay): Here at the mouth of bay it is like the congregation of all the fish that migrate south.

Despite all we know about migration – the mysteries of migration continue. Who knows where to go? Who knows when to go? Who knows how to get there? Some of the questions – even 3,000 years later – remain unanswered.

Elk Expert: My personal belief is that there's a lead cow somewhere in that matriarchal group that will just keep moving and then their calves follow.

Sandhill Expert: In my mind what happens here is the cranes are on their way north and they need a place to sit down and get all the energy they need to complete their migration.

We do know that Sandhill cranes have followed Nebraska's Platte River for more than 3 million years.

In truth, wildlife species that migrate do so to survive. But the trip itself can be full of danger.

Bird Expert: Probably the most important thing to realize is their ability to survive all the elements and do it so gracefully. They have a tendency to find the right places and eat the right things that can hold them over for their flight south to Mexico.

And this is a daily chore whether it be ice, rain or snow.

When these Franklin gulls head south from the Agassiz National Wildlife Refuge in northwest Minnesota, the journey ahead is, by any measure, remarkable.

Bird Expert: They are the longest migrating bird in the world. They migrate to the southwest coast of Chile so they have 3,000 miles to fly before winter sets in.

Indeed, feats of migration are almost beyond our comprehension. Long ago, scientists guessed that tiny hummingbirds hitched a ride on the backs of geese to go south. They were wrong, of course.

Today we know some migrating birds like mallards may fly at altitudes of 20,000 feet or more. We also know birds and animals are able to store fat energy to sustain their bodies for the rigors of the trip.

Sandhill Crane Expert: The Platte River is safety – its wide, it's shallow, it's a perfect place for them to roost at night and the corn fields around provide almost all the food that they need.

On Africa's plains, herds of wildebeest and zebras may take 250 mile journeys twice a year.

In the arctic, caribou herds are known to walk 350 miles in 10 days.

Even the monarch butterfly, so light and delicate, travels 2,000 miles in 60 days.

And who would guess this small duck, the Bluewing Teal, is capable of flying 3,800 miles in one month? Daily average? 125 miles a day.

From Orca whales to King Salmon. From Bald Eagles to backyard robins. From v-shaped goose flights to night flying coots. These are among the wonders of migration. And wonders never cease.

W

X

Y

Z

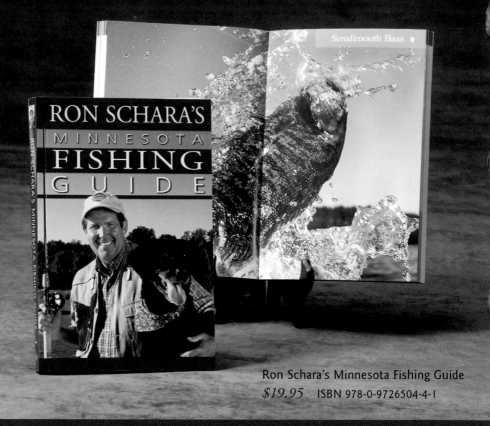

Ron Schara's Minnesota Fishing Guide
$19.95   ISBN 978-0-9726504-4-1

Ron Schara's Minnesota Fishing Guide

Anglers throughout Minnesota and beyond will be delighted to learn that noted outdoorsman and author Ron Schara has an award-winning Fishing Guide available. Ron Schara's Minnesota Fishing Guide is an exceptional guide to fishing in Minnesota that gives tips and techniques that are useful for the beginner as well as experienced anglers.

Ron Schara's Minnesota Fishing Guide contains tidbits from Raven, useful how-to information and the ONLY hard copy of vital Minnesota DNR lake statistics. The book contains full-color photos, technical drawings and highlights every major fish species found in Minnesota.

You can find Ron Schara's Minnesota Fishing Guide at local book, gift and sporting goods stores. You can also find the popular book online at **www.tristanoutdoors.com**.

TRISTAN OUTDOORS